LEARNING AMERICAN SIGN LANGUAGE
IN HIGH SCHOOL

LEARNING AMERICAN SIGN LANGUAGE IN HIGH SCHOOL

MOTIVATION, STRATEGIES, AND ACHIEVEMENT

Russell S. Rosen

Gallaudet University Press
WASHINGTON, D.C.

Gallaudet University Press
Washington, DC 20002

http://gupress.gallaudet.edu

© 2015 by Gallaudet University
All rights reserved. Published 2015
Printed in the United States of America

Library of Congress Cataloging-in-Publication Data

Rosen, Russell Scott.
Learning American sign language in high school : motivation, strategies, and achievement/Russell S. Rosen.
    pages cm
ISBN 978-1-56368-642-9 (paperback) – ISBN 978-1-56368-643-6 (e-book)
1. American Sign Language—Study and teaching (Secondary)—United States. 2. Sign language—Study and teaching—United States. I. Title.
HV2476.4.R67 2015
371.91'246–dc23
2015001655

∞ This paper meets the requirements
of ANSI/NISO Z39.48-1992 (Permanence of Paper).

To the students and graduates of the Program in the
Teaching of American Sign Language as a Foreign Language,
Teachers College, Columbia University,
New York, New York

Contents

	Preface	ix
	Acknowledgments	xi
1	Background	1
2	The Study	16
3	Motivation for Learning American Sign Language as a Foreign Language	30
4	Strategies for Learning American Sign Language	48
5	Learner Achievement	98
6	Conclusion	122
	References	129
	Appendix A	145
	Appendix B	149
	Index	153

Preface

Two issues provided the impetus for this book. One is the growth of programs and classes in American Sign Language (ASL) as a foreign language in United States (U.S.) high schools. The number of American high schools with ASL programs and classes increased 4000% between the first national survey conducted by the Center for Applied Linguistics in 1996 and a national survey that I conducted in 2005. The other issue is the dearth of studies on high school learners in ASL classes. In spite of the increase in ASL classes and programs in American high schools, little is known about the learners and how they learn ASL as a second language. No information is available to inform high school ASL teachers and program administrators on why learners take ASL for foreign language credit, how they learn new signs and grammar, and how their learning determines their achievement in ASL.

This book is based on a study that looked at the demographics, motivation, language processing, learning strategies, and course performance of two groups of learners (those with and without learning disabilities) in ASL as a foreign language class. More specifically, it examines the characteristics of the learners, the reasons they have for taking ASL, the way they process ASL as a language, their preferred strategies for learning the language, and their performance in ASL classes. Such information will help teachers and school administrators in their recruitment of future learners to ASL classes and in curriculum development and instructional planning.

The book begins with the historical background of teaching ASL as a foreign language in American high schools. This history includes the debates about the linguistic and foreign language status of ASL, the situation of deaf and hard of hearing learners in public secondary schools, governmental recognition of ASL as a language, and processes leading to its inclusion in the schools. The next section presents the findings of a national

PREFACE

survey of U.S. high schools that offer ASL for foreign language credit. The survey obtained information on the number and distribution of schools, teachers, classes, learners and departments, as well as the process for program implementation. The survey information was used to ascertain the current breadth and scope of these programs and to discern trends of ASL as a foreign language in public high schools nationwide. Some survey results were compared to available data on other foreign languages. Such comparisons helped determine the place of ASL in the foreign language domain within high schools.

This is followed by a discussion of issues in learning American Sign Language as a foreign language in high schools. The goal of education in a foreign language such as ASL is to ensure that the learners acquire the language and knowledge of the culture of the language users. Learners' achievement is associated with their motivation for learning the language, the way they process it, and the activities they devise to learn it. Motivation is tied to the learners' interest in the language, community, and culture of the language community. Language processing is governed by the perceptual schemas that learners rely on when thinking about the linguistic and extra-linguistic features of the language. Extra-linguistic features include discourse functions such as pausing to create topic boundary in narratives, and conversation implicatures such as turn-taking and forms of talk. Learning strategy is a learner-generated activity in which the linguistic and extra-linguistic features of the language are acquired and produced with information on the language, community, and culture of the foreign language users. This book seeks to investigate how motivation, language processing, and learning strategy variables of learning shape learners' learning and achievement in ASL classes. Results of this study may help teachers not only in developing strategies to showcase ASL when they recruit future learners to their classes, but also in creating learning activities that foster optimal learner achievement. Within each topical area of investigation is a series of studies of high school learners. The first section of each topical area covers learners who do not have learning disabilities, and the second section covers learners who have learning disabilities. Each topical part consists of an overview of theories on learner learning of foreign languages, a discussion of method, and the studies on learners' learning with results and analyses of the results. It concludes with a discussion of the studies and suggestions for teachers.

Acknowledgments

This book could not have been done without the support of my institution, Teachers College of Columbia University, and the five high schools that allowed me to conduct the research. My deepest-felt gratitude goes to the administrators and teachers at the school sites where the study was conducted. They were Mr. Russell Stewart, Headmaster, and Ms. Kimberly Braun, ASL Teacher, of York Preparatory School, New York, New York; Ms. Cristina DeFeo of Christ the King High School, Middle Village, New York; Ms. LauraAnn Weiss, Director, Languages Other Than English, and Ms. Allison Hynes, ASL Teacher, of Commack High School, Commack, New York; Mr. Kirk Smothers, Supervisor of High School, and Ms. Mary Kate DeLouise, ASL Teacher, of Mary McDowell Friends School, Brooklyn, New York; and Mr. Francesco Fratto, Assistant Principal for Languages Other Than English, and Ms. Laura Anderson and Ms. Antionette Waldner, ASL Teachers, of Half Hollow Hills High School, Dix Hills, New York.

My deeply-felt appreciation also goes to three individuals from the Gallaudet University Press. They are Ms. Ivey Wallace, for her patience and guidance in helping me go through the book preparation process, Ms. Deirdre Mullervy for preparing the book, and Ms. Jill Porco. Lastly and more importantly, my deepest-felt gratitude and much love goes to my late wife, Violet B. Stein-Rosen, who provided love, understanding, and encouragement for me to complete this book.

LEARNING AMERICAN SIGN LANGUAGE
IN HIGH SCHOOL

1

BACKGROUND

In the last two decades, an increasing number of U.S. high schools have begun to offer ASL as an option to meet state foreign language requirements for graduation. A national survey conducted by the Center for Applied Linguistics (CAL) in 1996 showed that 17 (1%) of the 1,650 surveyed U.S. high schools with foreign language programs in 1987 offered ASL, and 33 (2%) in 1997 (CAL, 1997). This represented a growth of almost 100% in 10 years.

This growth of ASL as a foreign language in schools is part of a general trend in educational institutions in adopting ASL for admission and graduation purposes.[1] Welles (2002) studied foreign language enrollments in institutions of higher education and found that 552 undergraduate colleges and universities in 2002 offered ASL classes. Learner enrollment in ASL classes had grown from 1,602 learners in 1990 to 4,308 learners in 1995, 11,420 learners in 1998, and 60,849 in 2002 (Welles, 2002). The growth rates were 3,698% from 1990 to 2002, and 432% from 1998 to 2002. The Modern Language Association reported that in 2009 there were 91,763 students in ASL classes, which represented a growth of 16.4% from 2006 to 2009 (Modern Language Association, 2010), and 109,577 students in 2013 (Modern Language Association, 2015), which represented a growth of 19.4% from 2009 to 2013. In addition, Wilcox and Wilcox (1991) found that as of 1991, 48 U.S. colleges and universities accepted ASL as one of the foreign languages that meet the requirement for undergraduate admission. The number had grown to 66 in 1997 (Wilcox & Wilcox, 1997) and 171 as of 2014 (Wilcox, 2014). This represented a growth rate of 256% from 1991 to 2014.

The growth had its contested beginnings. The study of the linguistic structure of ASL did not begin until 1960 (Stokoe, 1960; Stokoe,

---

1. This section is an abridgment of my article, "American Sign Language as a Foreign Language in U.S. High Schools: The State of the Art," which appeared in the *Modern Language Journal*, 92(1): 1–38.

Casterline, & Croneberg, 1965). By the 1970s and 1980s, ASL had been declared as a unique language by several linguists (Baker-Schenk & Cokely, 1980; Klima & Bellugi, 1979; Liddell, 1980; Padden, 1981; Valli & Lucas, 1992; Wilbur, 1979). Linguists generally found that ASL, in spite of its distinct visual modality, carries several linguistic features that are similar to spoken languages (Fischer & Siple, 1990; Fromkin, 1988; Neidle et al., 2000; Sandler & Lillo-Martin, 2006). However, the "discovery" of ASL as a language was followed by arguments, particularly among government officials and school administrators, regarding whether ASL really was a language and whether it should be offered for foreign language credit in schools (Armstrong, 1988; Belka, 2000; Caccamise, Garretson, & Bellugi, 1981; Cooper, 1997; Fromkin, 1988; Sinnet, 1995; Wilcox, 1992; Wilcox & Wilcox, 1997).

The arguments against ASL were based on the visual-manual nature and the geographical scope of ASL, and the disbelief in the existence of the community and culture of signing deaf people. Some government and education officials understood it to be either a manual representation of English or a sophisticated form of gestures and pantomimes. Others felt that learning ASL was easier than learning spoken languages because it was in the manual form (Peterson, 1999; cf. Shroyer & Holmes, 1982). In addition, ASL was created in the U.S. and is used largely by American deaf people. As such, ASL was not seen as "foreign." The reasoning was that foreign languages originate in countries outside of the U.S., and foreign language learners can visit the countries, use their languages, and study their cultures (Armstrong, 1988). In the case of ASL, there is no foreign country to go to in order to use the language (Belka, 2000; Reagan, 2000).

Another argument against ASL in schools was that the existence of a separate Deaf community is problematic. Some government and education officials considered deaf people as Americans and users of English. Their community is a subgroup of the larger American society, and its culture a subculture of American culture (Terstriep, 1993). Yet another argument against ASL was that it has no written form (Wilcox & Wilbers, 1987). This is unlike spoken foreign languages offered in high schools as they have both written and spoken forms. A final argument was that there is no cultural tradition in the Deaf community. All spoken foreign languages offered in schools carry a rich body of artistic and literary traditions that learners can study. As ASL does not have a written form, government

BACKGROUND

and education officials argued that ASL cannot have artistic and literary works nor possess cultural traditions (Wilcox & Wilbers, 1987).

The above arguments were counteracted by supporters of ASL as a foreign language (Battison & Carter, 1981; Chopin, 1988; Corwin & Wilcox, 1985; Wilbers, 1987, 1988; Wilcox, 1992; Wilcox & Wilbers, 1987; Wilcox & Wilcox, 1991, 1997). The supporters devised arguments based on linguistic, psycholinguistic, sociological, and anthropological research on ASL and the American Deaf community and culture. The arguments that ASL is a manual or gestural form of English were countered by studies in ASL linguistics that pointed to phonological, morphological, and syntactical similarities and differences between ASL and spoken languages (Liddell, 1980; Fromkin, 1988; Neidle et al., 2000; Sandler & Lillo-Martin, 2006; Valli & Lucas, 1992). ASL contains, for instance, phonological binary opposites, morphological combinations, and word order that are comparable to the features and constructions of the world's spoken languages. The arguments that ASL has no cultural traditions because it lacks a written form were dispelled by several researchers who found that there is a rich body of cultural traditions in the arts and literature that are recorded on videotapes (VHS), digital video devices (DVDs), and other visual media (Davis, 1998; Frishberg, 1988; Rutherford, 1988; Padden & Humphries, 1988, 2005; Wilcox, 1992; Wilcox & Wilcox, 1997). Histories of Deaf people and their language, community, and culture have been researched since the 1980s (Baynton, 1996; Gannon, 1981; Lane, 1984; Padden & Humphries, 2005; Van Cleve & Crouch, 1989) and showed that the Deaf community has not only been created but is also evolving. Deaf culture has been investigated as a sociocultural phenomenon of deaf people containing ideologies, artifacts, and social structures that revolve around ASL, visualism, manualism, deafness, and deaf-hearing relations (Lane, Hoffmeister, & Bahan, 1996; Padden & Humphries, 1988, 2005).

Furthermore, the argument that ASL is not a foreign language is based on previously-held perceptions of the terms "foreign," "nation," and "community." These perceptions have been altered by changes in the international geopolitical situation. Migration by people speaking different languages and carrying different cultures across geographic regions has broken down ties between language and nation. This leads to the concept of language use by a "community" of users, versus a "nation" of users. Individuals

CHAPTER 1

not using the language of the community are considered as "foreign" and their language as a "foreign language" (Armstrong, 1988; Wilbers, 1987). For individuals not born or enculturated into a given linguistic community, the language needs to be learned (Reagan, 2000; Wallinger, 2000). The idea that ASL is easy to learn compared to spoken languages because it is used in a manual-gestural form, had been dispelled by Shroyer and Holmes (1982), Kemp (1988), and Peterson (1999). Kemp (1988) conducted a study of the difficulties that beginning learners who speak have with learning ASL and found that the difficulties lay in the change in language processing modality. Learners needed to shift away from their oral-aural languages and process ASL visually. As such, ASL is as difficult to master as any spoken language. Since ASL shares universal linguistic principles with spoken languages (cf. Neidle et al., 2000; Sandler & Lillo-Martin, 2006), learning ASL may aid learners in mastering other languages (Kemp, 1989; Peterson, 1999). For supporters of ASL as a foreign language, the evidence of ASL linguistics and Deaf community and culture in scholarly and literary studies, along with post-colonialist notions of "foreign" in languages and communities, have superseded the arguments of ASL as a "manual-gestural representation" of English and that language is solely a product of user nationality. The recognition of ASL as a language and arguments in support of ASL as a foreign language empowered scholars and advocates from the Deaf community to seek its adoption as a foreign language worthy of study by state education departments and high schools.

I conducted a study in 2006 that outlined the history of the inclusion of ASL and Deaf community and culture in high schools. Through an examination of educational and historical documents, it was found that the impetus for introducing ASL for foreign language credit in public high schools was the presence of signing deaf and hard of hearing (D/HH) learners in classrooms (Rosen, 2006). The mainstreaming was initially framed by the Individuals with Disabilities Education Act (IDEA) practices that favored speech and hearing for learners with deafness. The Education for All Handicapped Children Act (EAHCA) (89 Stat. 773), passed in 1975, was one of the earliest U.S. federal laws that mandated the education of children with disabilities in public schools. The law established two definitions for deafness. "Deaf" refers to children who are unable to use any hearing to receive classroom information. "Hard of hearing" refers to children who can utilize hearing with amplification to receive information.

BACKGROUND

Now renamed as the IDEA (20 U.S.C. Section 1400–1487), the EAHCA sets as one of its goals the integration of deaf and hard of hearing individuals into American society. This integration happened by placement of D/HH learners in classrooms with hearing learners. Before these laws were passed, most D/HH learners were placed in special schools for the deaf. Schools for the deaf use sign languages, ranging from Manually Coded English to ASL, as the main means of communication. It was hoped that by placing D/HH learners in classrooms with hearing learners, D/HH learners would acquire the hearing and speaking communication skills that are needed to interact with hearing learners, so that they could ultimately be mainstreamed effectively into the American society. From 1977 to the present, D/HH learners have increasingly been placed in public school classrooms with hearing learner peers: 46% of D/HH learners were placed in public schools in 1977–1978, 61% in 1987–88, 88% in 1999–2000, and 91% in 2002–2003 (Gallaudet Research Institute, 2004a).

However, the mainstreaming of signing D/HH[2] learners in American schools created communication and language barriers between the D/HH and hearing learners in public education classrooms. Studies since the passage of the laws have consistently showed a lack of opportunities for interaction between signing D/HH learners and their hearing teachers and peers in public schools (Foster, 1989; Gaustad & Kluwin, 1992; Stinson & Liu, 1999). This communication situation of signing D/HH learners received attention from advocates, researchers, and the American Deaf community. They fought over the definitions, evaluation, instructional program, and placements of D/HH learners concerning communication needs and language preferences, thus making the implementation of the IDEA a debate between differing ideologies about how D/HH learners should be educated (Rosen, 2006).

Deaf community advocates, particularly representatives from the National Association of the Deaf (NAD), a national advocacy organization of deaf people in the U.S., held meetings with representatives from the U.S. Congress and officials from the U.S. Department of Education, a

---

2. Deaf and hard of hearing learners in mainstreamed settings exhibit diversity in communication preferences. Their languages range from speech and Cued Speech, to Manually Coded English and ASL. The "signing D/HH learners" refers to a subset of the deaf and hard of hearing learner population who predominantly use ASL.

cabinet-level entity of the U.S. government charged with the responsibility of implementing federal education laws and overseeing education practices in the nation. Deaf community advocates sought to alter notions of deafness and educational practices regarding language use in classrooms, placement, diagnosis, and evaluation (Rosen, 2006). The result of the meetings was a reconceptualization of deafness for educational purposes. In the 1997 and 1999 reauthorizations of IDEA, and the formerly-named EAHCA (1975) language was revised by deleting references to speech and hearing difficulties and their role in receiving linguistic information, and by including ASL as one of the "language preferences" of D/HH learners in the law for the first time (U.S. Department of Education, 1999). As a consequence of these changes in the IDEA language, public schools found it difficult to ignore sign language, including ASL, as a primary language and preferred mode of communication for the learners (Rosen, 2006).

Another change that came with the altered IDEA language was the increased presence of sign language interpreters with signing D/HH learners in mainstreamed settings. Their presence has increased since 1999, from 22.1% in 1999–2000 to 22.9% in 2001–2002, and 23.4% in 2002–2003 (Gallaudet Research Institute, 2004a). Their presence has generated interest among hearing learners and teachers in the lives, experiences, language, community, and culture of signing D/HH learners (Rosen, 2006). Hearing learners and teachers have increasingly requested courses in ASL and about the American Deaf community and culture (Rosen, 2006). As a result, general education schools accepted ASL as one of their languages. The presence of signing D/HH learners and the hearing learners' demand for classes in ASL have set into motion the creation of courses and programs in ASL as a foreign language in public schools (Rosen, 2006).

State legislatures and education departments needed to provide official approval so schools could offer ASL courses, which would include information on the Deaf community and culture, for foreign language credit. Beginning in the 1980s, members from the Deaf community initiated the process for meeting with and securing approval from state legislatures and state education departments. However, the process varied across states. Different sources within states initiated the process for implementing state recognition of ASL for foreign language credit in schools,

BACKGROUND

as Pfeffier (2003) found for Virginia, Loux (1996) for Nevada, Rosen (2005) for New York, and Selover (1988) and Clary (2004) for California, but followed a similar process for all in-house program and course approval (Clary, 2004; Pfeffier, 2003). In some states, the NAD, in collaboration with the American Sign Language Teachers Association (ASLTA), a leading American organization of teachers of ASL, met with state education departments and state legislatures and received approval (Rosen, 2006). In New York State, for instance, the Empire State Association of the Deaf, a state chapter of the NAD, several representatives from the state chapter of ASLTA, and other community leaders met with members of the state legislature, received approval, drew up curriculum and assessment materials, and devised examinations for teacher certification and learner diplomas (Rosen, 2006). In other states, community members and faculty from colleges and universities carried out the process. In California, a consortium of individual members of the Deaf community, such as the California Association of the Deaf, educational institutions such as California State University at Northridge, and community organizations, initiated the process (Selover, 1988). In Maryland, Nevada (Loux, 1996), Texas, and Washington, consortia of community organizations and leaders also initiated similar processes. In a few states, the process began at the political level. For instance, a memorandum written by the superintendent of schools, a top state education official, in Virginia in 1988 led to the passage of a resolution recognizing ASL as a foreign language in the state assembly in 1998 (Pfeffier, 2003; Wallinger, 2000).

As a result of Deaf community mobilization, the number of states that have formally recognized ASL as a foreign language has grown from 28 states in 1997 (Kreeft-Peyton, 1998), to 32 in 1999 (Jacobowitz, 1999), 38 in 2004 (Gallaudet Research Institute, 2004b) and 45 as of 2014. The number of recognizing states had grown 61% in 14 years since Kreeft-Peyton's (1998) study. One state, Delaware, had ASL legislation pending as of 2014. State legislation for ASL had never been proposed in 4 states also as of 2014. However, the offering of ASL for foreign language credit in high schools was not predicated on state education departments' recognition of ASL as a language. There were several states where ASL was not formally recognized, but their high schools offered ASL for foreign language credit. New Mexico and North Dakota are examples of

CHAPTER 1

states that had not formally recognized ASL as a foreign language, but high schools in these states offered ASL as a foreign language as of 2014. See figure 1 for the number of states recognizing ASL as a language. The rationale was that high schools offered foreign languages to help learners obtain college admission, which typically required at least two years of foreign language courses in high schools. In addition, there were some states, such as Alabama and Iowa, which formally recognized ASL as a foreign language, but none of their public high schools offered ASL foreign language classes. These states typically did not require foreign languages for any of its high school diplomas. In these cases, there was no relationship between state recognition of ASL and ASL offerings in its high schools. Therefore, there may be opportunity for an increase in the

Arizona	Kentucky	Ohio
Alabama	Louisiana	Oklahoma
Alaska	Maine	Oregon
Arkansas	Maryland	Pennsylvania
California	Massachusetts	Rhode Island
Connecticut	Michigan	South Carolina
Colorado	Minnesota	South Dakota
Florida	Missouri	Tennessee
Georgia	Montana	Texas
Hawaii	Nebraska	Utah
Idaho	Nevada	Vermont
Illinois	New Hampshire	Virginia
Indiana	New Jersey	Washington
Iowa	New York	West Virginia
Kansas	North Carolina	Wisconsin

States where recognition of American Sign Language is pending, as of 2014:

Delaware

States in which recognition of American Sign Language as a valid foreign language never proposed to state legislatures, as of 2014:

Mississippi   North Dakota
New Mexico   Wyoming

Figure 1. States that recognize American Sign Language as a foreign language, as of 2014.

BACKGROUND

number of high schools offering ASL for foreign language credit despite some state education departments' lack of recognition of ASL as a foreign language.

The results of Deaf community work in ensuring recognition of ASL and Deaf community and culture at the state government level carried over to public high schools (Rosen, 2006). However, high school principals, foreign language departments, and school districts needed to support implementation of ASL courses for credit to fulfill learner foreign language requirements in the schools. In addition, the high schools still needed to establish classes, enroll learners, and hire course teachers.

I conducted a survey in 2004–2005 to gather information about the schools, classes, learners, and teachers of ASL as a foreign language (Rosen, 2008). As mentioned, the survey's purpose was to ascertain the breadth and scope, and discern trends on ASL as a foreign language in public high schools nationwide. The specific topical areas for studying trends were the number and distribution of schools, teachers, classes, learners, and departments; types of curricula and instruction; and the process for program implementation (Rosen, 2008).

Lists of schools that offered ASL classes for foreign language credit were requested and obtained from U.S. state education departments in late 2004 and early 2005 for the survey. Of the 50 states sent the request, 38 states responded, and 31 states provided lists. Five states responded by saying that no high schools in their states offered ASL foreign language programs. Two other states responded, but did not provide lists. For these two states, an Internet search was conducted. However, this search was unreliable because of incomplete information, frequent website breakdowns, and invalid website hyperlinks while doing the searches. The 31 respondent states provided lists containing the names and addresses of close to 1,100 high schools with ASL foreign language programs. The lists included all types of high schools, including public, private, denominational, alternative, vocational-technical, specialized, and special education high schools. Due to financial and time constraints, the population of high schools with ASL foreign language programs was narrowed to a sample of public high schools.

Questionnaires were created that sought information on the number of public high schools offering ASL courses within a given state, the year

CHAPTER 1

ASL was implemented, the order of program establishment, learner enrollment, the number of teachers, types of training teachers received to become ASL teachers, the kinds of academic departments housing ASL classes, curricular materials and instructional approaches used by teachers, and the existence of ASL clubs by the academic year 2004–2005. The survey questionnaire is exhibited in Appendix A. Some survey information was requested for years other than the survey time period. In order to discern trends in learner enrollments, classes, and teachers, this information was requested for the 2002–2003 and 2004–2005 academic years. Information on program implementation was requested for the year of implementation. Information for the then-projected academic year 2005–2006 will not be discussed due to insufficient responses. In addition, survey data on curriculum and instructional approaches will not be discussed due to space limitations. Responses to the question about whether ASL was given foreign language credit in a high school or not were used to eliminate high schools that did not grant ASL foreign language credit from this analysis (Rosen, 2008).

Survey questionnaires were mailed in early 2005 to 628 schools in 31 states.[3] The response rates were 36% for respondents and 58% for the states in general. The responses were tabulated for analysis of trends. The following depiction of survey results is based on responses from 226 respondent schools in 18 states. Trends on the national number of public high schools with ASL foreign language programs, learner enrollments, classes, and teachers were based on information from respondent public high schools and were multiplied in proportion to the overall number of high schools in the respondent states to show the current status of ASL as a foreign language at the schools (Rosen, 2008). Figures for some states may be skewed due to insufficient responses from high schools and any interpretation of the results should take this into account.

Survey results showed that the total number of high schools with ASL foreign language programs and classes in the U.S. was 701 as of the 2004–2005 academic year for the 31 respondent states. These 701 high schools

---

3. The survey was made possible by financial and logistical support from the Department of Health and Behavior Studies, Teachers College, Columbia University.

BACKGROUND

represented less than 64% of all the 1,100 high schools, regardless of type, which responded to the survey (Rosen, 2008).

The 1997 CAL survey showed that 33 high schools offered ASL as a foreign language. The increase in the number of high schools with ASL programs in 2004 as compared with 1997 is over 2100%. Not every state had the same number of high schools with ASL programs and classes. Washington State had the highest number of such high schools, followed by Texas, Florida, California, Ohio, and New York. A few states had only one such high school. These states were Alaska, Michigan, Oregon, Pennsylvania, Vermont, Colorado, and North Carolina. Alabama, Delaware, Iowa, Tennessee, and Wyoming all have no high schools that offered ASL programs.

The number of high schools offering ASL for foreign language credit are meaningful only when compared with the number of high schools offering foreign languages in general. This comparison would help discern the number of these high school ASL programs, and would measure the extent of ASL penetration in high school foreign language programs. Unfortunately, it is not possible to discern relative sizes of ASL programs due to insufficient data about high school foreign language programs in general. No national statistics exist for the early 2000s about high school foreign language programs. Only the states of California and Indiana provided statistics about their high school foreign language classes during this period. California provided statistics on the number of schools, teachers, and foreign language classes at all levels, from kindergarten to high school. Indiana provided statistics on learner enrollments for all grades. However, these statistics were not sufficient in scope and, therefore, not helpful in assessing the extent of ASL penetration in American high school foreign language programs.

While the causal relationship between high school ASL programs and individual colleges granting foreign language credit for prior language study to fulfill admission and graduation requirements could not be discerned from this survey, increased high school enrollment in ASL classes seemed to parallel increasing college enrollment. As of 2005, about 150 national research universities accepted high school credit courses in ASL for admission purposes (Wilcox, 2006). Comparing the numbers between this list and earlier similar lists of Wilcox and Wilcox's (1997), it is clear that the number of such colleges and universities was growing. Increases in high school and college learner enrollments in ASL courses seems to suggest an increasing number of colleges and universities that grant foreign language credit for high school ASL courses.

Survey results are presented here regarding the questionnaire topics (Rosen, 2008). Respondents were asked about the number of learners enrolled in high school ASL foreign language classes for the academic years of 2002–2003 and 2004–2005. Survey results show that the number of learners enrolled in ASL classes nationwide had risen exponentially. Nationally, 56,783 high school learners enrolled in ASL classes during the 2002–2003 school year and 73,473 enrolled in such classes in the 2004–2005 school year. Learner enrollment in high school ASL courses rose 29.4% between 2002 and 2005. The states with the highest number of learner enrollments in the 2004–2005 school year were Texas, Florida, California, and Washington. The states with the fewest learner enrollments were Connecticut and Oregon. Almost all states, however, showed increases in learner enrollments. The states with the highest rate of increase in learner enrollments from 2002–2003 and 2004–2005 academic years were New Jersey, with a 212% increase, followed by Texas with a 51.7% increase, Utah with a 45% increase, Ohio with a 42.3% increase, and California with an increase of 37.4%. No state showed decreases in learner enrollment between the academic years 2002–2003 and 2004–2005 except for Virginia. Oregon showed a decline from 2002–2003 to the 2003–2004 school years, and Utah, Illinois, Maine, and Ohio showed a decline in 2004–2005 as compared with the 2003–2004 school years. Arizona and Connecticut exhibited no growth in learner enrollments across the same years (Rosen, 2008).

While the last two decades have seen exponential growth in ASL taught as a foreign language in U.S. schools, including elementary, high, and collegiate institutions (Wilcox, 2014; Rosen, 2008), it also saw an increasing number of learners with learning disabilities taking foreign language classes (Sparks & Javorsky 1999; Sparks, 2006), including ASL (Rosen, 2008). These learners taking foreign languages experienced learning disabilities, such as dyslexia and perceptual processing disorders. They were typically designated in the schools as "504" learners as defined in Section 504 of the U.S. Rehabilitation Act of 1973. This law mandated that public schools had to provide accommodations for learners with

BACKGROUND

disabilities. For learners with disabilities, federal regulations, such as the Individuals with Disabilities Education Act (IDEA), were the motivation for their enrollment into foreign language classes. The growth in ASL classes provided opportunities for learners with disabilities to interact with regular education learners.

According to respondents' comments in the survey, ASL courses attracted a relatively high percentage of learners with learning disabilities. These learners included those with deafness and other physical and learning disabilities. Table 1 shows the percentage of learners with learning disabilities taking ASL classes for foreign language credit. These percentages only cover the 2004–2005 school year.

Nationally, 13% of the learners in ASL classes were learners with learning disabilities (Rosen, 2008). Numerical variations across states can be seen in the percentage of learners with learning disabilities taking ASL

Table 1. Percentage of Learners Taking ASL Classes for Foreign Language Credit Identified as Learners with Learning Disabilities by State, for the 2004–2005 School Year.

State	Number of Special Education Learners, per State in the 2004–2005 School Year
Arizona	5
California	8
Connecticut	25
Florida	6
Illinois	10
Indiana	11
Maine	10
Maryland	1
Massachusetts	34
New Jersey	16
New York	15
Ohio	12
Oregon	15
Pennsylvania	N/A
Texas	14
Utah	10
Virginia	10
Washington State	9
National mean	13

Note: No school from the State of Pennsylvania provided information on the number of special education learners who take ASL classes.

classes. Massachusetts had the highest percentage of these learners in ASL classes, followed by Connecticut, New Jersey, New York, and Oregon. Maryland had the lowest percentage of learners with learning disabilities taking ASL classes, followed by Arizona and Florida.

However, the percentage of ASL learners who have physical and/or learning disabilities as compared with the total number of high school ASL learners could not be discerned from the survey. The impact of mainstreaming of D/HH learners in hearing classrooms on learning ASL and other languages could not be determined from the available survey results.

There was also an increase in the number of levels of ASL classes offered in public high schools during this period. Each course level corresponds to one year of study. For instance, if a learner's response is that they have taken 2 levels of ASL, it means 2 years of study. Respondents were asked about the number of levels of ASL classes for the 2002–2003 and 2004–2005 academic years. Survey results showed that the average number of levels of ASL classes has grown from 2.3 levels in 2002–2003 to 2.4 in 2004–2005 nationwide. This represented a growth rate of a little more than 4% from 2002 to 2005. In other words, an overall average of about two to two and a half years of study in ASL was offered in American public high schools. The states with the highest number of levels of ASL classes in the last school year of the survey, 2004–2005, were Pennsylvania, with four levels, followed by Utah with more than three levels, and Virginia and Texas with close to three levels. Connecticut had the lowest number of levels of ASL classes, with one level, followed by Maine, with close to two levels. The states with the highest rate of increase in the number of levels of ASL classes from the 2002–2003 to 2004–2005 academic years were Maryland with a 100% increase and California, Washington, New York, and Indiana with a range of 13% to 17% increase. Some states, such as New Jersey and Utah, showed declines in the number of course levels. A few states, such as Connecticut, Massachusetts, Oregon, and Pennsylvania, exhibited no growth (Rosen, 2008).

To sum, there has been growth in the number of high schools that offer ASL for foreign language credit since 2000. There were increases in the number and distribution of ASL programs, number and levels of classes, and number of ASL teachers and D/HH learners in public secondary schools in the 2002 to 2005 academic years covered in this survey.

BACKGROUND

Survey results suggest that the schools drew teachers largely from deafness-related teaching programs to teach ASL. The teachers needed to understand ASL, ASL and English linguistics, second language acquisition, ASL curricula, ASL instructional methods, and assessment forms and procedures, and know about the history, sociology, and anthropology of Deaf community and culture, and ASL and Deaf arts and literature. Teachers of children who are deaf and hard of hearing and signing D/HH people were the original creators of the idea that ASL was a valid foreign language to be taught in public high schools (Rosen, 2006).

2

THE STUDY

The growth in ASL classes in schools has sparked interest among second language (L2) researchers about hearing learners taking ASL classes for foreign language credit. The studies conducted up to the survey period under discussion had largely focused on college learners, however. No study of high school learners, specifically general education learners and learners with learning disabilities, had been conducted until this survey period. Information about the motivation for language learning processes, and achievement of high school learners in ASL classes were not known. ASL teachers need to understand these factors so they can develop curricula that reflect the survey findings for their learners.

Issues in Learning American Sign Language as a Foreign Language

The increase in learner enrollments in high school ASL classes behooves us to seek reasons for learners taking ASL to fulfill school foreign language requirements. This will inform ASL teachers about what to expect regarding learner language acquisition and how learning about the given linguistic community will appeal to learners. This information also will aid program planners, including school administrators and teachers, in curriculum development and recruitment of future learners.

Students learning ASL develop learning strategies to process and develop literacy skills in ASL so they can discuss different topics. What is not known is how learners think about and process newly learned signs and grammar. While there were studies in spoken L2 languages that looked at these factors, there had been no study about high school ASL learners to date. ASL teachers might need to adjust their instructional strategy to accommodate different learner learning styles.

THE STUDY

The ultimate goal of foreign language education is learner achievement. Researchers have conducted L2 spoken language studies that explored and assessed motivation and thinking and learning strategies factors as possible determinants for learner foreign language course performance. ASL teachers need this information to maximize learner achievement in their classes.

Several research questions were posed in this study:

1. What are high school learners' motivations for taking ASL as a foreign language?
2. Are there differences in learners' motivation by age, gender, and ASL course level?
3. What are the thinking strategies, or language perceptual processing schemas, favored by learners of ASL as a second language?
4. What are the learners' preferred strategies for learning ASL?
5. Which motivation and perceptual language processing strategies are predictors of learners' preferred ASL learning strategies?
6. Which motivation, language perceptual processing schemas, and learning strategies correlate with learners' final grades in these ASL courses?

This book looks at both general education learners and learners with learning disabilities in L2 ASL courses. Issues examined here are similar for both groups of learners, except no inquiry was made as to learning motivations for learners with learning disabilities. This was because there were a small number of respondents from one of the high schools and learners with learning disabilities were limited in their choice of foreign languages in the school. Questionnaires were developed and used to assess learners' motivation, language processing, learning strategies, and course achievement. It appears in Appendix B. Teachers were asked to submit final learner grades in ASL courses. Statistics were used to ascertain the relationship between questionnaire findings and foreign language performance by both learner groups.

Study Methods

Information was requested from several schools regarding survey focus areas mentioned above of general eduction learners and learners with learning disabilities. First, I contacted 9 schools to assess their interest level in participating in this research project.[4] Five schools, three of which served general education learners and two of which mainly served learners with learning disabilities, expressed interest. Negotiations followed on types of information asked of learners in the questionnaire, the schedule for learner completion of the questionnaire, and how the completed questionnaires would be given to me. The study schools agreed that the completed questionnaires and learner course grades would serve as my main information collecting sources from the learners. The schools requested that I conduct no interviews or have any interaction with the learners, and that only up to fifteen minutes would be given to learners for questionnaire completion.

Types of Schools Participating in the Study

General Education Learners

The three high schools with general education learners participating in the survey were located near New York City and were selected because they offered three ASL levels, or years, of courses for which foreign language credit was given. The schools were also selected because they differed in governance. One was a private, urban high school located in the Manhattan borough of New York City, the second was a public suburban high school in Long Island, New York, and the third was an inner-city denominational school in Queens, a borough of New York City.

In terms of governance, two of the three schools were both private high schools that charge their learners tuition. The public high school did not charge tuition. In addition, the public high school was a part of a school district in Long Island. The denominational school, while private, was administered by the Diocese of New York City. Another private school was independently run and has its own board of trustees and school administration.

---

4. The author makes no distinction between "foreign language" and "second language" within the confines of this study. The two terms are used interchangeably.

THE STUDY

The curriculum varied across the schools. The private high school offered a general education curriculum that included liberal arts and science courses, such as English, math, science, social studies, and foreign languages. The public high school also provided a similar general education curriculum. The denominational high school, also offered similar courses as the schools discussed above did. The school also offered religious courses in biblical studies, ethics, and ecclesiastical history.

Learner Residential Demographics

The neighborhoods in which the learners lived differed among the three schools. The private school was located in the Upper West Side part of Manhattan surrounded by apartments that were marketed in the six- to seven-figure price range. Most of the parents of the school's learners were affluent and earned at least six-figure incomes. The school also provided a few scholarships to learners from less affluent families. The neighborhood around the denominational high school contained single- and multi-family homes along with some apartments, mostly rental in nature, and its residents tended to be middle class. Neighborhood residents were largely Catholic and regularly attended church. Most of the parents of the denominational school learners averaged in the low-to-high five-figure incomes. The school attracted learners whose parents wanted their children to receive religious education. The public high school was in a suburban area of Long Island. The neighborhood around the school consisted of single-family homes with a scattering of apartments. Most parents of this school's learners were upper middle-class and earned incomes ranging from the high five-figures to low six-figures.

Types of Schools Participating in the Study

Learners with Learning Disabilities

Information about learners with learning disabilities came from two high schools located near New York City. One school was a public suburban high school in Long Island, with a contingent of learners with learning disabilities. The other was a private, special education high school in Brooklyn, New York, which served learners with learning disabilities only.

These schools were selected for this study because they offered ASL as a foreign language and its classes contained students that were diagnosed with learning disabilities.

The public high school did not charge learner tuition. In addition, it was a part of a public school district in Long Island that oversaw educational programs in its elementary, middle, and high schools. The private school was a special education school for learners with learning disabilities under the administration of Quakers in New York City. The private school was independent and had its own board of trustees and school administration, and charged learner tuition.

While both schools offered curricula that included traditional liberal arts and science courses, the private school in Brooklyn differed from the Long Island public school in that it also offered Quaker education coursework along with practical experiences in its traditional testimonies of simplicity, peace, integrity, community, equality, and service.

Learner Residential Demographics

The neighborhoods in which the learner body lived differed between the two schools. The private school in Brooklyn was surrounded by apartment homes that were marketed in low-to-high six-figure price range. The school's learners hailed from families of differing income levels. Some of the learners' parents were affluent and earned at least six-figure incomes, and they paid tuition to the school. There were also learners from less affluent families and they were given scholarships so they could also attend the private school. The public high school is located in Dix Hills, New York, where neighborhood families were affluent, surrounded by million-dollar homes. These learners' parents were upper middle-class to upper-class, and earned an average of high six-figure to low seven-figure incomes.

The private, special education high school in Brooklyn, New York, only offered ASL Level 1 classes during the time of the study, and the public high school in Dix Hills, New York, offered Levels 1 through 3 ASL classes, each covering Levels 1 through 3. The private school decreed that its learners with learning disabilities could only take ASL classes, not spoken foreign languages. By contrast, learners in the public high school

The Study

could decide which foreign language to take from a curriculum that offered ASL, Spanish, and Chinese foreign language courses.

The teachers of ASL classes in all high school study sites were hearing. They held Master's degrees and teacher certification from the New York State Education Department to qualify them as teachers of ASL as a foreign language. The teachers employed content- and task-based communication approaches in the teaching and learner learning of ASL. These teachers taught content that pertain to daily life, such as, but not limited to, personal information, home, family, education, food, leisure, employment, shopping, community, neighborhood, future plans, and that also included information about the Deaf community and culture. They constructed conversation exercises so the learners could develop ASL skills using signs and grammar when discussing various topics. Teachers also used pictures, images, and words to introduce concepts and linguistic principles about different topics. To these ends, the teachers developed several learning activities, including learner narration, dialogues, homework, games, project work, and sign and grammar exercises. The teachers largely employed the target language, ASL, and did not use their voices while teaching the learners. They at times have had to use the learners' native language, English, and speak, in order to help some learners understand signs and their relationship to concepts. The teachers graded their learners to indicate learner course performance. For this study, the teachers were not asked to modify their teaching strategies. The focus of the study was not on teachers' attitudes or pedagogical practices, but on their learners' motivation for taking ASL, language learning processes, and course achievement.

Survey Instruments

To answer the research questions, a questionnaire was drawn that included items covering demographics, motivation, and language learning process. Teachers provided learners' course grades. This study was prepared for and received approval from principals, assistant principals, chairpersons of LOTE, Languages Other Than English, a New York State Education Department designation for world, foreign, modern, and classical languages

Chapter 2

other than English. The study was initiated after receiving school approval from all study locations. As negotiated with participating high schools, the questionnaires were given to the teachers, who, in turn, distributed them to and collected them from the learners. The teachers either mailed or gave the completed surveys to me. Only learners and their parents who had signed study consent forms were given the questionnaires. Data for this study were derived solely from questionnaire responses. In the questionnaires, the learners were designated anonymously by using their birthdates as identifiers.

Questionnaire

A questionnaire consisting of 52 variable items was developed with several parts and Lickert-type responses for the learners without learning disabilities. The questionnaire appears in Appendix B. The parts included 10 items of learner demographic information, 15 items concerning learner motivation for taking ASL, 3 items about their perceptual processing of ASL, and 24 items about their ASL learning strategies. Responses to questionnaire items were self-reported by the learners.

Study Participant Information

The 10 items of demographic characteristics contained questions about age, gender, ethnicity, ASL level, first language spoken, number of languages spoken, whether the ASL course was required or an elective, and learner involvement with the deaf community. Based on learner responses, only demographic information on age, gender, and ASL level were subjected to further analyses. The item on the required or elective nature of ASL course was used to eliminate all responses from learner participants who took ASL as an elective from further analysis. This study only covered learners who took ASL as a required, not elective, course. The other demographic items mentioned above were eliminated from further analysis due to insufficient information.

Reasons for Taking American Sign Language

The second part of the questionnaire was entitled "Reasons for Taking American Sign Language." It consisted of 15 items on integrative and instrumental motivation. Learners' motivations and related study results are discussed in chapter 3.

The Study

Learning and Using ASL

In order to assess learner language processing and language learning strategies, another part of the questionnaire, entitled "Learning and Using ASL," was prepared with 27 items. These items and results are discussed in chapter 4.

To assess whether the questionnaire items measure the same constructs, a test for internal reliability and adequacy was employed. A Cronbach's Alpha Test was performed. The test assessed intercorrelations among the items. Maximal intercorrelations imply that the items measured the same constructs. The 42 items about motivation, language processing, and learning strategy in this study's questionnaire had the Cronbach's Alpha of 0.757, which indicated that the internal reliability of the questionnaire items was adequate.

The instrument used for the study of learners with learning disabilities was this same questionnaire, but modified. It contained only three parts, one part covering demographic characteristics, one part covering learners' language processing, and one part asking about learners' preferred language learning strategies. One of the participating schools for learners with learning disabilities required that its learners meet the foreign language requirement for graduation by taking only ASL courses. This, in effect, removed the utility of including items as to motivation in the revised questionnaire for these learners. Consequently, for learners with learning disabilities, this study focuses on the other research areas, namely the relationship between learner language processing and learning strategies, and their effect on learners' course achievement.

Grades

The ASL teachers provided me with their learners' ASL course grades that showed learner class performance levels. Learners' grades were based on how well they comprehended ASL in receptive examinations, signed production in expressive examinations, and paired conversation examinations; homework; in-class presentations; research projects; and attendance. This study did not include any analysis of learner language proficiency; instead, grade scores reflected language proficiency as measured in cumulative scores from receptive-comprehension and expressive-production examinations, homework, presentations, projects, and attendance.

Chapter 2

Study Learner Participants

General Education Learners

I received a total of 217 questionnaires from the three schools that enrolled only learners without learning disabilities. Seven questionnaires were eliminated for various reasons. Two of the questionnaires only included responses to questionnaire demographic items, but not on the other areas under study. One questionnaire contained insufficient responses to demographic items. Four questionnaires contained multi-responses to several questionnaire items, which made analysis difficult. In order to conduct meaningful statistical analysis, the decision was made for research purposes that questionnaires kept for analysis needed to contain single responses to all demographic items and at least answers to 43 out of 45 questionnaire items, or variables, about motivation, language perceptual processing, and learning strategy. This criteria yielded 210 valid questionnaires for further analyses after questionnaire answers not meeting this criteria were eliminated.

The participants in this study were high school learners without learning disabilities who took ASL courses for foreign language credit in school. The age range of the 210 learner respondents was 13 to 18 years old. The mean age was 15.2 years old. There were more females (61%) than males (39%) taking ASL for foreign language credit. This is similar to other study findings for learners taking college-level ASL classes (Miller, 1976; Lang et al., 1996; Peterson, 2009). This demographic information is also similar to studies concerning some learners taking L2 spoken foreign languages classes (Williams et al., 2002; Kissau, 2006). As is typical of foreign language classes, most learners were in Level 1 classes ($N = 95$) with the fewest number of learners in Level 3 ($N = 50$) classes. There were more white than non-white learners by a ratio of 2 to 1 in the ASL classes. Close to 80% of the learners spoke only one language prior to taking ASL, and more than 90% of this group spoke English as their first language. Table 2 summarizes these demographic characteristics of learners without learning disabilities of the student-participants of this study.

$N = 195$ learners without learning disabilities both took ASL courses and received final grades for foreign language credit by the end of the

THE STUDY

Table 2. Demographics of Learner Participants Without Learning Disabilities.

Category	Subcategories	N	% of respondents
Age	13	7	3.3
	14	63	30.0
	15	57	27.1
	16	47	22.4
	17	33	15.7
	18	3	1.4
Gender	Male	82	39.0
	Female	128	61.0
ASL Course Level	ASL 1	95	45.2
	ASL 2	65	31.0
	ASL 3	50	23.8
Ethnicity[a]	Whites	135	64.3
	Non-Whites[b]	72	34.3
Number of Languages Spoken[c]	One	167	79.5
	Two or more[d]	39	18.6
First Language Used[e]	English	190	90.5
	Other[f]	15	7.1

Notes:
[a]There are 3 missing cells for Ethnicity.
[b]Non-Whites include African-Americans, Hispanics, Asians, and Other.
[c]There are 4 missing cells for number of languages spoken.
[d]Two or more languages include Spanish, Italian, Russian, Estonian, and Other.
[e]There are 5 missing cells for first language used.
[f]Other languages include Spanish, Italian, Russian, Creole, and Other.

academic year. For the study of learner achievement and correlates, questionnaire responses and course grades received for these learners only were analyzed.

Learners with Learning Disabilities

The other high school study participants were learners diagnosed as having one or more learning disabilities and who took ASL courses for foreign language credit. There were N = 38 learners in the ASL classes.

Chapter 2

The questionnaire that appears in Appendix B asked participating schools about the type and number of disabilities of the learners in their ASL classes. This information is shown in Table 3. Figure 2 shows the abbreviations used for questionnaire items in tables 3 and 19–24 since the questions were too long to include in the tables.

Some learners had other disabilities in addition to a learning disability. For example, two of the learners had autism, one of which student each had speech and language impairments, and another one had a hearing impairment. Five students have a combination of the following disabilities: hearing impairments, Tourette's Syndrome, attentive disorder and hearing disorder, speech and language impairments, and fine and gross

Table 3. Gender and Disability Demographics for Learner Participants with Learning Disabilities.

Learner	Gender	Learning Disability	Learner	Gender	Learning Disability
1	M	Autism	20	M	SpchLangImp
2	F	learning disabilities	21	F	learning disabilities
3	M	learning disabilities	22	F	learning disabilities
4	F	ADD	23	F	learning disabilities
5	F	learning disabilities	24	F	OHI
6	M	Tourette's, ADD	25	F	learning disabilities
7	M	learning disabilities	26	F	learning disabilities
8	F	learning disabilities	27	F	learning disabilities
9	F	learning disabilities	28	M	learning disabilities
10	F	ESL	29	F	learning disabilities
11	M	ESL	30	M	learning disabilities
12	M	OHI, ADHD, FineandGrs	31	M	learning disabilities
13	M	OHI	32	M	learning disabilities
14	F	learning disabilities	33	M	learning disabilities
15	M	Autism, ADD	34	F	learning disabilities
16	F	learning disabilities	35	F	learning disabilities
17	F	learning disabilities	36	M	learning disabilities
18	M	learning disabilities	37	F	learning disabilities
19	F	learning disabilities	38	M	learning disabilities.

Notes:
Tourette's = Tourette's Syndrome
ADD = Attentive Deficiency Disorder
OHI = Other Hearing Impairments
ADHD = Attentive Disorder Hearing Disorder
SpchLangImp = Speech and Language Impairments
FineandGrs = Fine and Gross Motor Deficiencies

Perception = Language perceptual processing schema
IntellIntLang = Intellectual interest in the language
TakeUniqLang = ASL is a unique language that I want to learn.
TakeChallMys = I want to challenge myself in learning the language.
CareerPlans = Career Plans
TakeLearnDeaf = I want to learn about deaf people.
TakeWorkDeaf = I want to work with deaf people in the future.
TakeTeacherASL = I want to become an ASL teacher in the future.
EasyLearnLang = Ease of learning a foreign language.
TakeEasyLearn = It is easier to learn a foreign language.
TakeEngBetter = ASL helps me learn and use English better.
TakeFailOthLang = I did not do well in other foreign languages.
TakeCommFam = I want to communicate with my family.
ThnkPixImag = I think of pictures and images that describe the new signs.
ThinkActions = I think of actions that describes the new signs.
ThinkEngTransl = I think of its English translation.
NotePixImag = I draw pictures and images that describe new signs.
NoteActions = I put down actions that describes the new signs.
NoteEngWords = I put down English words for new ASL signs.
FrmL1EngWord = I think of English words when I learn new ASL signs.
FromL1EngSent = I think of English sentences when I learn new ASL sentences.
LrnWantASLEng = To have a combination of ASL and English spoken
LrnWantEng = To have as much English as possible spoken
LrnWantASL = To have only ASL signed
LrnGiveNarrate = I give narrations.
LrnDialogues = I do dialogues with other people in class.
LrnTextbook = I follow the students' textbook.
LrnListen(Watch) = I listen (watch) activities.
LrnGrammExer = I do grammar exercises.
LrnPlayGames = I play ASL games in class.
LrnHomework = I do homework.
LrnProject = I do project work.
LrnTransEngASL = I translate from English to ASL.
LrnTransASLEng = I translate from ASL to English.
AskTeacher = I ask the teacher.
AskStudents = I ask other students.
AskTextbook = I look up in the textbook dictionary, Internet, CDs, or videos.
LrnEmphVocab = I emphasize vocabulary.
LrnEmphGramm = I emphasize grammar.
LrnEmphDiscourse = I emphasize discourse.

Figure 2. Abbreviations of Questionnaire Items in Tables 3 and 19–24.

Table 4. Demographics for Learner Participants with Learning Disabilities.

Category	Subcategory	N	%
Age[a]	14	11	39.3
	15	12	42.9
	16	3	10.7
	17	1	3.6
Gender	Male	11	39.3
	Female	17	60.7
ASL Course Level	ASL 1	16	57.1
	ASL 2	9	32.1
	ASL 3	3	10.7
Ethnicity	Whites	21	75.0
	Non-Whites[b]	7	25.0
Number of Languages Spoken[c]	One	23	82.1
	Two or more[d]	4	14.3
First Language[e]	English	24	85.7
	Other[f]	3	10.7

Notes:
[a]There is 1 missing cell for age.
[b]Non-Whites include African-Americans, Hispanics, Asians, and Other.
[c]There is 1 missing cell for number of languages spoken.
[d]Two or more languages include Spanish, Italian, Russian, Estonian, and Other.
[e]There is 1 missing cell for first language.
[f]Other languages include Spanish, Italian, Russian, Creole, and Other.

motor deficiencies. This study focused solely on learners with learning disabilities, and not on those who also had other disabilities. The learners with more than one disability were eliminated from further analysis. This left 28 learner participants who only had learning disabilities. The study analyzed their questionnaire responses and course grades received. Other demographic information for these learners is shown in Table 4.

Data and Statistical Analysis

Statistical analysis was used to answer the research questions. Two different sets of statistics were employed, one for learners without learning disabilities, and the other for learners with learning disabilities. Factor analysis, discriminant analysis, and regression analysis were used to assess

The Study

clusters of variables into factors, its assignment to age, gender, and ASL level groups. These same analyses were also used to assess the significance in the relationship between demographic variables of age, gender, and ASL level with measures of motivation. These same methods were used in analyzing the learner motivational data from the learners without learning disabilities. For the study of language learning strategy, descriptive statistics and regression analysis were used to assess the relationships between learners' motivation, language processing schemas, and learning strategies. Statistics were also used to ascertain the strength of relationships between the independent variables of learner motivation and language processing schema, and the dependent variable of learning strategy.

Statistics also provided answers to the same research questions with regard to learners with learning disabilities. Because the focus of this study centered on learner learning disabilities and their effects on language processing, learning strategies, and course achievement, the statistics employed with this learner group were different from those used in the study of learners without learning disabilities. Descriptive statistics, K-Mean cluster analysis, and independent samples t-tests were used to assess the demographic characteristics of learner participants and the significance of the relationship between learning disabilities, language processing, language learning strategy, and learner course grades. The multilevel statistical analyses were conducted using the PASW (*Predictive Analytics SoftWare*, formerly *Statistical Package for the Social Sciences* [SPSS]) 18.0 computer program.

The following sections discuss the findings yielded by my assessment of the effects of learner motivation, language processing schemas, language learning strategies on learner course achievement. Previous studies in these areas are first reviewed, then are followed by this study's research findings concerning learners with and without learning disabilities in the discussion of each assessment area. The review of other studies on the learning of foreign languages, both spoken and signed, as second languages helps identify issues relevant to this study and provides other study results to compare with this study's findings. The book concludes with an overall discussion of the studies and, based on learner course achievement results, proffers suggestions for the recruitment of and type of pedagogy used with learners in ASL classes.

3

MOTIVATION FOR LEARNING AMERICAN SIGN LANGUAGE AS A FOREIGN LANGUAGE

The observation that the last two decades witnessed exponential growth in the number of ASL courses offered in U.S. schools—elementary and high schools, and collegiate institutions—attests to increased hearing learners' interest in learning the language (Rosen, 2008). This growth, in turn, generated an interest in the L2 research community about the reasons behind learner motivation for learning ASL as a foreign language. A number of L2 studies, therefore, examined motivation as an indicator of learner interest and as a variable that contributed to learner learning of ASL.

This research into learner motivation for taking ASL was part of an overall development of this construct within spoken foreign language studies since the 1970s. The spoken L2 research community saw motivation as a variable that contributed to learner interest, participation, learning, and persistence with foreign language classes. Gardner and Lambert (1959) provided the earliest construct of motivation from a socio-educational perspective, which was further refined in Belmechri and Hummel (1998), Gardner (2001), Ushioda (2001, 2003), Noels (2003), and Noels, Pelletier, Clement, and Vallerand (2000), into two aspects—integrative and instrumental—of motivation. Integrative, or intrinsic, motivation reflects a genuine interest in learning a second language by identifying with the language and culture of a linguistic community. Instrumental, or extrinsic, motivation pertains to a pragmatic interest in learning a foreign language without identification with a linguistic community. Examples of instrumental motivation are taking foreign language courses for gainful employment and for earning class credit. Gardner developed the *Attitude Motivation Test Battery* (AMTB) (Gardner 1985, 2006; Gardner & MacIntyre, 1993) with questionnaire items about integrative and instrumental motivation. Studies by several L2 researchers (Stewart-Strobelt & Chen, 2003; Noels, Pelletier, Clement, & Vallerand, 2000; Grosse, Tuman, & Critz, 1998; Ely, 1986; Shedivy, 2004) utilized and modified Gardner's scale into various forms and found that L2 learners take foreign language classes because of career plans and desire to communicate with native speakers of a foreign language. Other studies (Watzke, 1994) also found that L2 learners take foreign language classes due to graduation requirements and pressures from parents and significant others in their community. Since Gardner and Lambert's (1959, 1972) development of the integrative and instrumental motivation concept, other researchers have proposed more reasons behind learner motivation. Oxford and Shearin (1994) found that people take foreign languages because of intellectual interest in or fascination with aspects of a given language. Crookes and Schmidt (1991) added that curiosity drove people to take a foreign language. Noels et al. (2003) proposed a self-determination theory for both types of motivation. That is, taking a foreign language depends on person's self-concept, either ideal or ought-to in relation to the linguistic group (Dörnyei, 2001, 2003, 2005; Dörnyei & Csizer, 2002; Dörnyei & Ushioda, 2009). The presumption within these studies was that learners had different reasons and plans for foreign language study.

Several researchers have also conducted motivational studies of L2 ASL learners. Miller (1976), Lang, Foster, Gustina, Mowl, and Lui (1996), and Peterson (2009) conducted studies about the motivation, attitudes, and perceptions of hearing, adult learners in community education and college-level ASL classes. Miller (1976), in her survey of learners in college-level ASL classes, found that half of the learners stated personal reasons, and the other half indicated job-related reasons for learning ASL. The personal reasons given were a sense of personal challenge and an intellectual interest in learning a language of a different modality from spoken English. The job-related reasons given were career plans to become teachers of deaf people or become involved in church work with deaf people. Lang, Foster, Gustina, Mowl, and Lui (1996), in their study of motivation of collegiate-level L2 learners in ASL classes, also found that the reasons for taking ASL was to earn college credits, personal challenge, intellectual interest in the language, and a need and want to communicate and interact with deaf people. In addition, professional hearing people working with deaf individuals had job-related reasons for enrolling in ASL classes. Lang et al., (1996) also found that integrative motivation was positively correlated with cultural attitudes toward deaf people. Peterson (2009) studied college-level learner perceptions of deaf people along with these learners' language learning of ASL in their first ASL course at 13 American colleges and universities. He modified Horowitz's *Beliefs about Language Learning Inventory* (BALLI) (1988), which surveys learner perceptions about the task of language learning, into *Beliefs about Learning ASL Inventory*. Results of Peterson's survey, indicated by percentages below, showed reasons learners had for taking ASL. They were for general interest (48%), improving English skills (40%), receiving academic credit (15%), assisting with career plans (18%), and a need for communicating with family and friends (7%).

In addition, a number of studies in L2 spoken languages showed demographic variations among learners in their motivation for taking foreign languages. One set of studies looked at the relationship between gender and motivation. Williams, Burden, and Lanvers (2002) discovered that girls were more integratively motivated than boys in taking French as a foreign language class. French was being seen by males as feminine. Kissau (2006) added that male learners lacked interest in studying French as a second language because of societal- and classroom-related pressures. Boys reported they felt less capable than girls in French classes because they perceived that society did not value men taking French classes. Mori and Gobel (2006) found that males and females scored equally on tests of intrinsic motivation. However, their findings showed that female learners had a greater interest in the cultures and people of the target language community, had more of a desire to make friends with the people in the linguistic community, and were more interested in traveling and/or studying abroad than were male learners. Male learners, on the other hand, were more concerned about employment and course credit. These findings were replicated in Dörnyei and Clement (2001) and Baker and MacIntyre (2003). Apparently, the mixed results on gender and motivation in the above L2 spoken language studies suggest that the relationship between gender and motivation is inconclusive.

A number of studies were conducted on the gender of college learners taking ASL courses. The studies nonetheless showed that more females than males take ASL classes. Miller (1976) found that 78.3% of females took ASL classes versus 21.7% of males, which supports this finding. Peterson (2009) also found that more females (80.4%) than males (19.6%) took ASL classes, a similar finding to Miller's study. Miller and Peterson did not provide reasons for the disparity in percentages of males and females who took ASL classes. These studies were limited to college learners, however.

Other studies in spoken L2 learning looked at the relationship between learner grade level and motivation, and still others explored the relationship between learner age and motivation. Kormos and Csizer (2008), in their study of European high school and university learners of English as a foreign language, found that motivation varied across different learner groups. High school learners were interested in cultural products created in English-speaking countries, and the university and adult education learners were interested in gaining their standing in the international arena such as the arts, finance, trade, and political affairs where English is largely spoken. MacIntyre, Baker, Clement, and Donovan (2003), in their study of junior high school learners, found that grade level, not gender, correlated with learners' integrative motivation. There was a decline in integrative motivation in higher grade levels. Gardner and Smythe (1975) in their study of high school learners, found that grades 7 and 11 learners exhibited more positive attitudes toward learning foreign languages than did learners in grades 8, 9, and 10. Ghenghesh (2010) investigated the temporal dimension of L2 motivation and found that, in contrast to Gardner and Smythe, L2 integrative motivation in the sample learner groups decreased with age. Ghenghesh explained that teachers shaped learners' attitudes toward and motivation for learning foreign languages. The learners' attitudes and motivation were negatively affected over time when their teachers were found to be strict with them, had insufficient contact with language community, and favored and provided motivation to certain learners who share the same ethnic nationality as the teachers (Ghenghesh, 2010).

The L2 spoken language studies reviewed above also showed demographic variations among learners in their motivation for taking foreign languages. While these studies covered high school learners, ASL studies at the time covered largely college-, graduate- and professional-level program learners. The studies also included subjects from different educational institutions. There are no studies to date before this one that had compared ASL learners' motivation of those from different high school settings within a locale. For this study, the research interest is in the motivation that American high school learners have for taking ASL for foreign language credit. This study also inquires whether learner motivation varies by age, gender, or ASL course level. Results from this study will be compared with findings from previous studies of both high school learners of spoken languages and college learners taking ASL. Implications of the results for the relationship between learners and motivation, and strategies for recruitment of future ASL learners are discussed in the conclusion.

Research Method

The research questions posed in the previous chapter pertain to the relationship between types of learners who took ASL for foreign language credit, their motivation for taking ASL, their preferred language perceptual processing schemas, their preferred language learning strategies and their course achievement. In the learner questionnaire (see Appendix B), the 10 items concerning learner demographics and the 15 items regarding learners' motivation for taking ASL are analyzed here. The second part of the questionnaire, "Reasons for Taking American Sign Language," explores learner motivation for taking ASL. Two questions about motivation were posed in this section—"Why do I take ASL?" and "I take ASL because . . ." Under each question several answer choices were given that included a mix of 10 integrative and 5 instrumental motivation constructs.

I examined motivation constructs from Gardner and Lambert's *AMTB*, Horwitz's *BALLI*, and Peterson's *Beliefs about Learning American Sign Language* studies and reports on motivators by Lang et al., (1996), Oxford and Shearin (1994), Crookes and Schmidt (1991), and Belmechri and Hummel (1998) for guidance on developing the motivation items. The number and length of the items in the questionnaire were constrained by two conditions. One condition was that the schools allowed only a limited amount of time for learners to complete the questionnaire. Another condition was that the questionnaire introduced unique topics specifically relevant to learning ASL as a language, D/HH people, and the learning of

ASL, as reported by Lang et al. (1996) and Peterson (2009). ASL learners used English as their L1 and might only have had a limited understanding of these concepts. Due to these constraints, the wordings of and the length of items in the various scales present in the Lang and Peterson studies mentioned previously could not be used. The questionnaire items, therefore, were shorter in length. Nonetheless, the questionnaire was built on the orientation constructs with integrative and instrumental reasons that were developed by Gardner and Lambert (1959, 1972), Horowitz (1988), and Peterson (1999) along with previous similar studies. The sources of the motivation items in the questionnaire are shown in Figure 3.

Building on concepts of motivation developed in previous studies, questionnaire items were modifications of the items in several scales. The integrative items relied on Gardner's (1988, 2006) *AMTB*'s integrative orientation constructs that emphasized learner desire to learn ASL, about deaf people, and the ability to interact with ASL-using communities. The instrumental motivation items came from the *AMTB*'s instrumental orientation constructs that emphasized the pragmatic value of learning ASL (cf. Gardner & Lambert, 1985, 2006; Gardner & MacIntyre, 1993), such as learners seeking employment that necessitated their working with D/HH individuals or pressures on them from families and school authorities. The *AMTB*'s motivational intensity construct also provided items on future plans to study and use ASL. In addition, Peterson's (2009) and Horwitz's (1988) studies provided other constructs that particularly pertain to the learning of foreign languages. Peterson modified the *BALLI* by substituting "ASL" for "foreign languages." His scale accounted for the unique nature of ASL as a language. Questionnaire items reflected this. In the *BALLI*, Horwitz mentioned the difficulty in learning a foreign language and included teacher suggestions to learners that they take a foreign language that would be "easier to learn" (Horwitz, 1985). The questionnaire also included items that related to the motivation construct of intellectual interest in a foreign language on which the Crookes and Schmidt (1991) and Oxford and Shearin (1994) studies focused. Items related to future career plans as a motivation construct was drawn from Gardner and Lambert (1959, 1972). The motivation constructs of wanting to work with D/HH people and/or becoming an ASL teacher were borrowed

Question	Motivation Item	Motivation Construct	Source
Why do I take ASL?			
	Intellectual interest in the language	Integrative	Crookes and Schmidt; Oxford and Shearin
	Ease of learning a foreign language	Integrative	BALLI
	Need to communicate with family and friends	Integrative	AMTB
	Career Plans	Instrumental	AMTB
I take ASL because			
	It is easier to learn than other foreign languages.	Integrative	BALLI
	ASL is a unique language that I want to learn.	Integrative	Oxford and Shearin; Peterson
	I want to communicate with my family.	Integrative	AMTB
	I want to communicate with my friends.	Integrative	AMTB
	I want to learn about deaf people.	Integrative	AMTB
	I want to challenge myself in learning the language.	Integrative	Oxford and Shearin
	ASL helps me learn and use English better.	Integrative	ACTFL
	I want to work with deaf people in the future.	Instrumental	Belmechri and Hummel
	I want to become a teacher of ASL in the future.	Instrumental	Belmechri and Hummel
	I did not do well in other foreign languages.	Instrumental	BALLI
	My guidance counselor asks me to take ASL.	Instrumental	AMTB

Figure 3. Summary of motivation items in relation to motivation constructs.

from Belmechri and Hummel (1998). Finally, the American Council on the Teaching of Foreign Languages (ACTFL), a leading organization of researchers, administrators, and educators in foreign languages, suggested that schools emphasize the idea that learner learning of foreign languages would aid them in developing better English literacy skills (ACTFL, 1993). This motivation construct was also included in the questionnaire to find out if this was a learner motivation for learning ASL.

Likert-type responses were employed in the questionnaire. The responses used were "most important," "somewhat important," "least important," and "not important." They were coded in numerals for statistical analysis. A test for internal reliability and adequacy was used to assess whether the questionnaire items measure the same constructs, the result of which is shown in a later section.

Only general education learner responses to the motivation items were analyzed. As indicated earlier, motivation data for learners with learning disabilities came only from one school and there were too few learner respondents to conduct meaningful statistical analysis. In the other school, learners with learning disabilities could only take ASL as a foreign language, rendering learner motivation irrelevant. Therefore, their motivations were not analyzed.

Study Results

For this study, the interest in motivation is to determine the reasons learners without learning disabilities have for taking ASL for foreign language credit and whether different learner groups have similar or different reasons for studying ASL. This information may be crucial for teachers as they develop instructional materials for ASL courses. This also may be helpful to teachers in their recruitment efforts to give reasons why learners might want to take ASL classes. Results of learner responses to questionnaire items on motivation are shown in Table 5.

Most learners marked the following reasons as "most important" and "somewhat important" in their motivation-related responses. These reasons include intellectual interest in the language, the perceived ease of learning ASL, the uniqueness of ASL as a language, taking ASL as a personal challenge, the need for communicating with family and friends,

CHAPTER 3

Table 5. Motivation of Learners Without Learning Disabilities Taking ASL Courses.

Motivation	Degree of Importance Answer Choices			
	Very	Somewhat	Least	Not
Intellectual interest in the language	55.2	39.5	4.3	1.0
ASL as a unique language to learn	72.4	20.5	3.8	3.3
Personal challenge in learning the language	46.7	33.8	11.0	8.5
Future career plans	4.8	13.4	23.0	58.9
Learning about deaf people	43.3	37.1	13.3	6.2
Working with deaf people in future	17.7	29.2	34.4	18.7
Wanting to be an ASL teacher	7.7	15.8	29.2	47.4
It is easier to learn a foreign language	33.3	43.3	18.6	4.8
ASL helps learners learn and use English better	9.0	15.2	29.0	46.8
ASL is easier to learn than other foreign languages	29.0	31.0	20.5	19.5
Not doing well in other foreign language classes	16.3	10.5	16.7	56.5
Guidance counselor suggests that learner take ASL	1.4	0.5	4.3	93.8
The need to communicate with family and friends	55.2	39.5	4.3	1.0
Desire to communicate with family	4.8	5.2	16.2	73.8
Desire to communicate with friends	9.0	14.3	21.0	55.7

Note: Table 5 data is in percentages.

and the desire to learn about signing D/HH people. Most learners marked the following reasons for motivation as either "least important" or "not important." These reasons include not doing well in spoken foreign languages, taking ASL to better learn English, future career plans, teacher and guidance counselors' suggestions that they take ASL, needing to communicate with family and friends in ASL, the desire to work with D/HH people, and wanting to become ASL teachers.

High school learners varied in their responses to questionnaire items on motivation. The question at hand is whether learners marked different items for motivation on the questionnaire. If they all agreed on the importance of a questionnaire item, learners were not differentiated by the item. If the learners varied in their responses to an item, they are said to be differentiated by the item. A factor analysis was performed to identify motivation variables that may account for that differentiation. Factor analysis reduces motivation variables into factors, each consisting of clusters of variables based on intercorrelations. Factor analysis was performed for all learner respondents. The resulting factors were then subject to further analysis. Variables not intercorrelated with others were eliminated from further analysis. Varimax rotated factor loadings were conducted to discern results for learner motivation variables. The parentheses refer to factor loadings. Only the items of >0.40 are included. The factors cover 66.955% of variance. The sampling, as measured using Kaiser-Meyer-Olkin Measure of Sampling Adequacy, is 0.762, which is adequate. Bartlett's Test of Sphericity: Chi-Square $\times 2$ (120) = 1178.387, p < .000.

The factor analysis of learner responses to questionnaire items on motivation generated five factors for learners to take ASL as a foreign language. Factor 1 is labeled generally as "career plans." Its three motivation variables are career plans (.826), wanting to work with D/HH people (.820), and wanting to teach ASL (.833). Factor 2 is labeled generally as "the uniqueness and challenge of ASL learning." The two variables included are seeing ASL as a unique language (.760), and learners challenging themselves in learning it (.801). Factor 3 is labeled generally as "the need to communicate with family and friends." The variables in this factor relate to the need (.904) and desire to communicate with family (.818) and friends (.515). The factor 4 variable is learners taking ASL to improve English skills (.938), and the factor 5 variable is the learner not doing well in other foreign languages (.974). This factor is labeled generally as "performance in other foreign languages."

Do different groups of learners vary in their reasons for taking ASL for foreign language credit? The next task was to discern motivation differences among high school learners by age, gender, and ASL course levels. In order to find differing motivation factors for these study criteria, a discriminant analysis was performed. Discriminant analysis tests how well factors predict membership of factors to groups and the degree of variance in learner responses. The first analysis of this data was to determine how well the five motivation factors predicted high school learners' membership in age, gender, and ASL course level groups. Table 6 shows the results.

Chapter 3

Table 6. Summary of Discriminant Functions for General Education Learners' Motivation by Age, Gender, and ASL Course Level.

Function	Eigenvalue	Wilk's Lambda	Chi-Square	%Variance	Cumulative%	p
Age						
1	.159	.657	82.087	35.7	35.7	.010
2	.128	.761	53.305	28.9	64.6	.078
3	.087	.859	29.723	19.6	84.3.	.327
4	.051	.934	13.387	11.4	95.7	.644
5	.019	.981	3.705	4.3	100.0	.813
Gender						
1	.216	.822	38.628	100.0[a]	100.0	.000
ASL Course Level						
1	.193	.790	46.444	76.1	76.1	.002
2	.061	.943	11.615	23.9	100.0	.312

Note:
[a] According to this statistic, the other gender plays no role and contributes 0% variance in learner motivation.

Eigenvalues and Wilk's Lambda are given for each factor.[5] Table 6 shows that only Function 1 significantly differentiated learners into age, gender, and ASL level groups. It ascertained a 36% of learner response variance for age, 100% for gender, and close to 80% for ASL course level. Functions 2 through 5 did not significantly differentiate learners into age groups nor did function 2 for ASL course level groups. In addition, the significance levels for function 1 for age, gender, and ASL course level were small enough to be the function that differentiated learners into age, gender, and ASL course level groups. The significance levels for functions 2–5 for age and function 2 for ASL course level were not small enough to be the function that differentiated learners into these same

---

5. For each factor, eigenvalue represents the variance in learner responses that is explained by that particular factor. Wilk's Lambda shows the variance in learner responses that are accounted for by each factor. The higher the lambda is, the smaller the within-group variability and the higher the differences in group means among learners for each factor.

MOTIVATION FOR LEARNING ASL AS A FOREIGN LANGUAGE

Table 7. Factor Loadings on Significant Functions for General Education Learners' Motivation by Age, Gender, and ASL Course Level.[a]

Factor		Function 1	Function 2
Age			
	I want to become a teacher of ASL in the future	.700*	
Gender			
	Career plans	.471	
ASL Course Level			
	ASL helps me learn and use English better.		−.426*
	I want to work with deaf people in the future.	.413*	
	I want to become a teacher of ASL in the future.	.697*	

Notes:
[a]Derived from structure matrix.
*Largest absolute correlation between each variable and any discriminant function.
Only correlations of > 0.40 are shown.

groups. Because functions 2–5 for age and function 2 for ASL level did not significantly differentiate learners into age and ASL course level groups, all motivation factors within these functions were excluded from further analysis of membership of learners in subgroups within age, gender, and ASL course level groups.

The second part was to identify which of the motivation factors by survey participants served as functions that differentiated them into age, gender and ASL level groups. Data from a structure matrix of variables on the significant functions was used.[6] Table 7 shows results of factor loadings on motivation variables for each of the significant motivation functions by age, gender, and ASL course level groups. Results indicate which variables had the highest loadings and served to differentiate participants according to age, gender, and ASL level groups. Correlations of more than 0.40 and functions that significantly differentiated learners into age, gender, and ASL course level groups are only shown (Fields, 2005).

---

6. The structure matrix consists of pooled within-groups correlations between discriminating variables and standardized canonical discriminant functions. Variables are ordered by absolute size of correlation within function.

CHAPTER 3

Table 8. Functions at Group Centroids for General Education Learners' Motivation by Age, Gender, and ASL Course Level.

		Function
Learner Groups		1
Age	13	.459
	14	.346
	15	.195
	16	−.352
	17	−.647
	18	.688
Gender	Male	.578
	Female	−.370
Course Level	ASL 1	.472
	ASL 2	−.350
	ASL 3	−.463

Notes: Lowest scores indicate response of highest importance to questionnaire item. Highest score indicates response of lowest importance to questionnaire item.

Table 7 shows that Function 1 differentiated learners into age, gender, and ASL course level groups. The highest loadings, regardless of the '+' or '−' values, were taken for interpretation of factors. The table suggests that function 1 for age and ASL level groups covered factor 1, the variable of wanting to become an ASL teacher. Function 1 for gender is the career plan variable. Table 7 results may indicate that only career plans differentiated learners into age, gender, and ASL course level groups. Based on the loading value, the factor that differentiated learners in the ASL course level groups was that learners did not take ASL classes because ASL would help them learn and use English better.

The next step was to find membership of motivation functions for subgroups within age, gender, and ASL course level groups. A group centroid calculation was performed.[7] Table 8 shows functions at group centroids for motivation within these groups.

The direction of distance from zero indicates the type of learner responses. A negative score indicates the direction of responses to "most

---

7. Group centroids consist of mean function scores of each group. The further the scores are from zero, the greater the difference between mean function scores between groups.

Motivation for Learning ASL as a Foreign Language

important," and a positive score indicates the direction of responses to "not important." Table 8 shows that for age groups, 17-year-old learners agreed that becoming a teacher of ASL was the most important motivator for them to take ASL, and 13-, 14- and 18-year-olds agreed that it was of no importance. This study found that the learners in each age group were motivated, but for different reasons.

In addition, this study found that females said that the desire to work with deaf people in the future was the most important motivator for their taking ASL, and males said that it was not. Learners in ASL 3 classes said that the desire to become a teacher of ASL was the most important motivator and learners in ASL 1 classes said that it was not important. All other motivation variables did not differentiate learners into age, gender, and ASL course level groups and subgroups. This is to say that the other variables were not the motivators for whole classes of age, gender, and ASL level, although they may have been motivators for individual learners.

Discussion

The above results show the five most important motivation factors high school learners have for taking ASL as a foreign language. They are an intellectual interest in the language, career plans, a need to communicate with family and friends, a need to improve English skills, and not doing well in other, spoken foreign languages. The study found that the motivation factors were similar to motivations indicated in previous studies conducted by Miller (1976); Lang et al. (1996); Peterson (2009); Watzke (1994); Stewart-Strobelt and Chen (2003); Noels, Pelletier, Clement, and Vallerand (2000); Grosse, Tuman, and Critz (1998); and Ely (1986). More particularly, the motivations were similar to those of high school learners of spoken foreign languages studied by Stewart-Strobelt and Chen (2003); Noels, Pelletier, Clement, and Vallerand (2000); Grosse, Tuman, and Critz (1998); Ely (1986); and Shedivy (2004). High school learner motivations in this study were similar to those of college learners taking foreign languages (Shedivy, 2004). Also, high school learner motivations for taking ASL were similar to those of college learners taking ASL classes (Miller, 1976; Lang et al., 1996; Peterson, 2009). The motivation items of career plans, guidance counselor course suggestions, and not doing well in

CHAPTER 3

other foreign languages were not similar to those indicated in these prior studies. These three motivators may be unique to high school learners. College learners often take foreign languages in connection with their majors and/or future career plans. Also, college department advisors have different roles from high school guidance counselors and that motivation is irrelevant.

This study found that the learners in each age subgroup were motivated for different reasons. The data show, for example, that 17-year-old learners said that becoming an ASL teacher was the most important motivator for them taking ASL. By contrast, the 13-, 14- and 18-year-old learners said that it was not an important motivator for them. These results contrast with Ghenghesh's (2010) finding that L2 motivation decreased with age.

This study found that more female learners than male learners took ASL because of future career plans. This agrees with findings in other ASL learner studies conducted by Miller (1976); Lang et al., (1996); and Peterson (2009). This study found that females said that their desire to work with deaf people was the most important motivator for them to take ASL but this motivator was not important to males. The fact that female learners in this study showed more interest in working with deaf people as a community of language users, are consistent with the findings of Mori and Gobel (2006), Dörnyei and Clement (2001), and Baker and MacIntyre (2003). They found that female learners have a greater interest in the people and culture of a given linguistic community than do male learners. Whether male learners saw ASL as feminine language, similar to the boys in the Williams, Burden, and Lanvers (2002) study in which the boys saw French as a feminine language, and that of Kissau (2006), who found that boys were not pressured by society to take French, may be a supposition that requires further investigation.

Previous studies of ASL learner motivation (MacIntyre, Baker, Clement, & Donovan, 2003; Gardner & Smythe, 1975) found that as junior high school learners progressed to higher ASL class levels, their motivation for taking ASL decreased. By contrast, this study found that no decline in motivation occurred in ASL learners in all course levels. This study found, rather, that learners taking differing ASL level courses within and across schools had different motivations for doing so. Learners in higher ASL course levels said that the desire to become an ASL teacher was their most important motivator, while learners in ASL 1 classes said that it was not important to them.

One finding on learner motivation—that learners took ASL as a part of their career plans to work with signing deaf and hard of hearing individuals—attests to the increased sensitivity of the learners toward the wealth of culture and community activities of the deaf and hard of hearing signing populace. Several studies show how foreign languages help enhance learners' appreciation of the diversity of the world's cultures, to see the variations in language structures, and to be able to embark on careers with members of the foreign-speaking communities (American Council on the Teaching of Foreign Languages, 1999; Gardner & Lambert, 1959, 1972). If ASL as a foreign language was offered, that if some learners took it as a part of their curiosity about the language, community and culture of signing deaf and hard of hearing people, and that learners took ASL for the same reasons as learners of spoken languages, then that attests to the success of ASL as a foreign language. ASL courses benefited learners in that it increased their understanding of underrepresented language minorities and their cultural sensitivity to these experiences.

This study provides several findings about the value of ASL for hearing learners. ASL provided the learners with career possibilities and also alternate ways to express their thoughts. Most of the learners had not been exposed to ASL and to the rich world of the Deaf community and culture prior to taking ASL. ASL provided some learners with a possible avenue for their career work with deaf and hard of hearing individuals and, as a result, an increased involvement in the language, community and culture of Deaf and hard of hearing individuals. A number of learners took ASL because they did not perform well in other (spoken) foreign languages. Their choice may suggest that they were visual processors of languages. That some learners took ASL to improve their English skills suggest that they hoped that ASL had the potential to aid them in imagining and organizing concepts needed for more clear communication in English. In addition, some learners had family and friends who sign. Taking ASL enabled them to communicate more with family and friends.

CHAPTER 3

Implications for Learner Recruitment

Results from this study also have implications for the recruitment of future high school learners taking ASL for foreign language credit. Taking into consideration learner motivation factors identified in this study, ASL teachers need to incorporate them into their lesson plans to attract future learners to ASL. Teachers need to match motivators to learners' interests and plans. Each motivator is discussed as to the implications for the recruitment of future learners and learners by age, gender, and ASL course level.

Some learners took ASL because they wanted to work in deafness-related careers. For targeting these learners, teachers should showcase the merits of ASL as a language with a community of ASL users, and put forth possible future careers working with signing Deaf and hard of hearing people. Teachers may want to invite Deaf and hearing people in the fields of interpreting, education, psychology, social work, and the humanities to speak with learners about deafness-related careers. Teachers may want to take these learners to colleges and universities with a sizable contingent of deaf learners, such as Gallaudet University in Washington, D.C, the National Technical Institute for the Deaf in Rochester, New York, and California State University at Northridge to see what careers aspiring teachers, interpreters, social workers, and psychologists are working in and to speak with them on career requirements and planning.

Some learners were attracted to ASL because of its linguistic uniqueness and wanted to challenge themselves by learning it. These learners may have been attracted to ASL because it is a visual language, which may match their preference for processing information visually rather than aurally. Teachers may want to show how the visual processing of information will aid learners better than auditory processing of it in comprehending concepts covered, not only in ASL classes, but in other academic subjects such as math, science, English literature, and history as well.

Other learners were attracted to ASL because they did not perform well in other spoken foreign languages. These learners first need to be identified. These learners may not have done well due to their weakness in processing information given in auditory format. In addition, they may

MOTIVATION FOR LEARNING ASL AS A FOREIGN LANGUAGE

have experienced difficulties with English literacy generally because of poor auditory processing skills. ASL teachers may need to emphasize to these learners that ASL as a visual language may aid them in language processing and help them improve their English literacy skills. These learners may need persuading to take ASL to help them understand linguistic concepts that may, then, aid them in mastering English and other spoken foreign languages and as a way of meeting foreign language requirements needed for graduation.

Other learners may have wanted to communicate in ASL with their relatives and either to maintain or strengthen their relationships with family and friends. ASL teachers may want to invite learners who sign with their families and friends to speak to these ASL learners about their experiences with this and of the merits of learning and using ASL to strengthen familial ties and friendships. In addition, some of these learners may have deaf babies in the future and will need to know how to communicate with them. Based on research that show that early linguistic and cognitive access to language for infants are enhanced through ASL (e.g., Mayberry, Lock, & Kazmi, 2002), parents who are armed with knowledge of and skills in ASL may be the most capable people to foster the linguistic and cognitive development of their future infants, and give them a healthier psycho-social environment than other parents.

The next chapter examines the relationship between high school learners' language perceptual processing schemas and learning strategies. The first part discusses language perceptual processing schemas and language learning strategies. The second part examines motivation and language processing schemas as possible predictors of learners' language learning strategies.

4

STRATEGIES FOR LEARNING AMERICAN SIGN LANGUAGE

Language Learning

Language learning consists of processing language and developing learning strategies to better understand it. Language processing entails thinking about the perceptual saliency of words and sentences for understanding linguistic form and meaning. Language learning strategies means that teachers must use materials and activities that will aid learners in their understanding and communication of the language in all its forms and meanings. This part looks at the thinking and learning strategies of secondary school ASL learners.

Thinking Strategies: Language Processing Schemas

Learners' thinking strategies for processing a language is another learner variable that shapes their foreign language learning. Language processing is an act of thinking about a language and its linguistic and extra-linguistic features. The brain processes information in various ways, using perceptual modalities such as sight, hearing, touch, smell, and taste. It subsequently converts the obtained information into knowledge (Keefe, 1979, 1987; Letteri, 1988). Foreign language processing is understood in L2 research as consisting of learners' preferred modality through which to receive and think about the phonological, lexical, and syntactical attributes of a language (Dunn & Dunn, 1983; Horwitz, 1994). In other words, perceptual language processing relates to the sensory modality that learners prefer to use in processing the linguistic and extra-linguistic features of a language.

LEARNING ASL AS A FOREIGN LANGUAGE

Learners' preferred perceptual modality may be one or many sensory modalities (Barbe & Swassing, 1979). Barbe and Swassing (1979) and Dunn and Dunn (1983) identified three perceptual modalities most relevant in the classroom, and they are visual, auditory, and tactile/kinesthetic. If a learner processes language visually, the learner prefers to see the language being used. If a learner processes language aurally, then the learner prefers to learn by hearing the language. If a learner processes language kinesthetically, then the learner prefers to learn it by acting on ideas or manipulating objects.

Learners were found to vary in the perceptual modality they use to process linguistic and extra-linguistic information. In a summary of prior studies on perceptual learning styles of learners, Dunn and Dunn (1988) found that less than 30% of learners preferred to process information aurally, 40% of learners preferred to process information visually, and the rest either kinesthetically, visually-tactually, or a combination of the visual and tactile. While Barbe and Swassing and Dunn and Dunn studied learners in non-foreign language classes, their findings may shed light on how learners' perceptual processing of language shapes their overall processing of language.

Language Learning Strategies

If learners study a foreign language, the presumption exists that learners are interested in learning linguistic and extra-linguistic features of a language. It is also presumed that learners are interested in learning about the community and culture of its native users. Learners use learning activities to acquire this linguistic and cultural knowledge.

Language learning includes activities that learners use to learn a language and develop literacy skills so they can talk about topics. This is collectively termed as language learner strategy (LLS). LLSs are a set of activity responses to problems in learning within social context and/or inside the heads of learners to help them comprehend, learn, or retain new information (O'Malley & Chamot, 1990; Oxford, 1990b, 1993; Dörnyei, 2003). Instruments were created to assess learners' learning strategies. Two of these are Horwitz's *Beliefs about Language Learning Inventory (BALLI)* (1988) and Oxford's *Strategy Inventory in Language Learning (SILL)* for foreign languages (Oxford & Burry-Stock, 1995) that contain cognitive, metacognitive, affective, and social learning strategies.

L2 literature has identified several learning strategies that the L2 learners preferred to use in foreign language classes. Naiman et al. (1978) proposed pragmatic strategies that included task approach, realization of language as a system, means of communication, affective management, and performance monitoring as learner strategies. Wong-Fillmore (1979) offered some social strategies used in language learning, such as communication strategies and strategies for identity management. O'Malley and Chamot (1990), building on the work of Anderson (1983, 1985) argued for a cognitive view of human thought and action and proffered cognitive strategies, including metacognition (planning, monitoring, and evaluating processes), cognition (processing), and social (affective and social) strategies. Oxford (1990) and Oxford and Burry-Stock (1995) further refined LLSs into linguistic strategies. These linguistic strategies contained direct strategies, which included memorization, cognitive, and compensation strategies, and indirect strategies, such as metacognitive, social, and affective strategies. The above studies identified several learning strategies and agreed that they all pertain to the cognitive, linguistic, pragmatic, affective, and social aspects of learning.

The use of several LLSs by ASL learners was studied by Peterson (2009), who conducted a survey of college-age learners in 13 U.S. colleges and universities learning ASL as to their motivation, attitudes, and learning strategies used. He modified Horwitz's *BALLI* survey into a *Beliefs about Learning American Sign Language* Inventory in his study. Peterson (2009) found in his study of these learners that most learners (60.4%) preferred that the use of both spoken English and ASL serve as the vehicle for learning ASL. Seventy-five percent of learners thought that grammar instruction was important. About half of the learners thought that learning vocabulary was important. Most learners (63.4%) preferred to ask teachers if they had questions. The results suggest that most of the ASL learners in Peterson's study preferred to learn ASL vocabulary and grammar, that both spoken English and ASL are used to learn ASL, and that they would ask their teachers if they had questions.

Studies also examined the difficulties L2 learners encountered in learning ASL and proffered several explanations. McKee and McKee (1992) and Peterson (2009) conducted studies on ASL learners' experiences learning the language. McKee and McKee (1992) studied learners and teachers in ASL course levels 3 to 5 in a university program. Most learners in the study were in the university's Deaf Studies program. McKee and McKee asked them to rank aspects of learning ASL in terms of degrees of difficulty, ranging from 1 for easy to 6 for most difficult. They found that learners expressed ASL learning difficulties in the areas that received a rating of 3 or more based on the unique features of the language. These areas were thinking in ASL, expressing thoughts easily in ASL, mastering grammar and syntax (such as word order, pronoun deletion rules), mastering hand-eye-body coordination (such as eye contact, manual dexterity, visual acuity, use of nonmanual segments, and spatial indexing), and developing fluency. Kemp (1998) added that ASL learners' learning difficulties were due to their weak visual and manual processing of ASL, poor uses of L1 language structures to help organize their ASL signing, overall negative and domineering social attitudes toward signing D/HH people, misconceptions of ASL as a system of icons and a manual representation of English, and lack of acculturation, or cultural immersion, into the signing D/HH community. Peterson (2009) also found in his survey that learners also expressed difficulty learning ASL for which he offered several explanations. These included learners' nervousness in using ASL, problems in visually attending to teachers, poor visual acuity and manual dexterity, their teachers' negative attitudes, and insufficient opportunities for practice.

That ASL learners had found difficulties with learning the language may be explained by the investment they put into learning, including motivation and processing of the language. However, no study existed until this one on how ASL learners' motivation for and linguistic perceptual processing of ASL shape the way they learn it. This relationship was studied in L2 research on spoken foreign languages. The interest in L2 research lies, along with instruction and resources, in how the learner variable of motivation for taking a language and beliefs about the language and the language community influence language learning strategies. This study attempts to fill that gap. Implications of the study for pedagogy and future research are discussed later.

This study looks into how learner motivations for taking ASL as a foreign language and the way they process ASL may determine their preferred learning activities. As a part of their investment in language learning, learners needed to have a purpose for taking ASL and a way for processing the language. It is possible that these aspects of how learners learn ASL have influenced their learning of the language. In pursuance of this, the study investigates motivation and language perceptual processing predictors of learners' learning strategies. The L2 spoken language research community conducted studies as to how these factors have shaped learners' use of learning strategies.

Relationship between Motivation and Learning Strategy

The relationship between motivation and learning strategy was investigated in several studies. The studies found that learners' strategy use is correlated with motivation (Nyikos & Oxford, 1993; Oxford & Nyikos, 1989; Mochizuki, 1999; Wharton, 2000; Chou, 2002). Okada, Oxford, and Abo (1996) found that metacognition, cognition, and social strategy use correlated with high motivation. Chang and Huang (1999) investigated the relationship between learner motivation, both integrative and instrumental, and learning strategies for English as a foreign language (EFL). They found that different learning strategies were associated with different types of motivation. Integrative motivation was associated with cognitive and metacognitive learning strategies, and instrumental motivation was associated with memory and affective strategies. Social strategies have had little relationship to either integrative and instrumental motivation. Nakayama (2005) and Chen (1999) showed that learners who had high ratings on scales of integrative motivation preferred to use metacognitive, pronunciation, and organization strategies. While limited to spoken second languages, the studies showed that learners' motivations do influence their learning strategies for learning. Up to the date of this study, there was no study on the relationship between motivation and learning strategy in L2 ASL.

Relationship between Language Processing Schemas and Learning Strategy

The next issues to consider was the relationship between language processing and learning strategy, and the effect of motivation and language

LEARNING ASL AS A FOREIGN LANGUAGE

perceptual processing on learning strategy. More particularly, the study looks at whether learning strategies are associated with learner motivation for learning ASL and the perceptual processing they employed when doing this. Unfortunately, no study existed before this one about the relationship between language processing and learning strategy in ASL. There are, however, studies regarding this relationship in spoken foreign languages.

Several studies of spoken foreign language learning found that students' preferred perceptual processing schema were associated with their preferred learning strategies. (cf. Dunn & Dunn, 1983). Horwitz (1994) and Dörnyei (2005) found that learners who visually processed a language, for instance, wanted to receive information through sight. They performed learning activities that required sight for information retrieval. These activities included reading, seeing images, pictures, diagrams and maps; looking at concrete objects; imagining mental pictures; and highlighting with bright colors to make information more visually salient. Oxford (1995a) found 50% to 80% of foreign language learners in North America used visual perceptual processing schema. Other researchers distinguished between visual and verbal learners. Visual and verbal learners focused on written words, and visual but nonverbal learners focused on images (Kinsella, 1995). Learners who preferred the auditory perceptual processing of languages wanted to receive information through hearing. They performed learning activities that required hearing for information retrieval, such as listening to lectures, role plays, oral directions, audio tapes, recitation, and conversation (Dörnyei, 2005; Oxford, 2003). Between 20% and 40% of learners used the auditory perceptual processing schema (Dunn & Dunn, 1978; Reiff, 1992). Oxford (1995a) added that a relationship existed between gender and perceptual language processing. Oxford (1995a) found that more women than men were auditory learners. Learners who preferred the kinesthetic modality for processing a language wanted to receive information through body movements, either in parts or whole. They performed learning activities that require bodily actions for information retreival, such as walking, carrying, riding, building objects, and role-play (Kinsella, 1995a; Kroonenberg, 1995; Dörnyei, 2005). Oxford (1995a) found that more men than women, as well as many underachieving and culturally disadvantaged learners, were kinesthetic-tactile learners (Reiff, 1992). As mentioned earlier, other learners may have employed multiple perceptual modality schemas when learning languages (Barbe & Swassing, 1979; Dörnyei, 2005; Keefe, 1987).

The focus of this study is on the perceptual schemas that high school learners use for processing ASL and in the ways they think while doing so. The perceptual schemas identified in the previous studies are visual, auditory, and kinesthetic. The issue of interest here is whether the high school learners in this study processed ASL signs and sentences by thinking visually, aurally, and/or kinesthetically. Learners who processed ASL through the auditory modality when learning new signs and sentences may think in English. Learners who processed ASL through the visual modality when learning new signs and sentences may think in pictures and images. Learners who processed ASL signs and sentences through the kinesthetic modality may think in terms of actions.

Relationship between Motivation, Language Processing Schemas, and Learning Strategy

Unfortunately, no study existed until this one that assesses the relationship between motivation, language perceptual processing, and learning strategy in either spoken or signed languages, including ASL. This study examines the effect of learners' motivation for learning and processing ASL on their selection of learning strategies used in ASL courses.

Issues of Processing and Learning American Sign Language for Learners with Learning Disabilities

This section examines high school learners with learning disabilities who took foreign language courses as to their preferred language processing schemas and language learning strategies. Issues were raised, however, regarding these learners' learning of foreign languages. Studies showed that learners identified as having learning disabilities and who took native language classes experienced difficulties learning the native language. The question is whether the identified and assessed learning difficulties in native languages carried over into foreign languages for these learners.

LEARNING ASL AS A FOREIGN LANGUAGE

Studies discovered that learners with learning disabilities having difficulties in learning native languages also have had difficulties in learning foreign languages, particularly in regard to spoken foreign languages. Dinklage (1971) identified foreign language learning problems of learners with learning disabilities in the areas of reading and writing, listening and oral communication (speech), and memory problems for sounds and words (overlapped with listening difficulties), and for knowledge and information retrieval. More specifically, learning disabilities that made learning foreign languages difficult for this population were phonological, orthographic, speaking, listening, memory, and comprehension. Learners with learning disabilities tended to reverse and omit letters and letter sequences (ei vs ie) when spelling words. They also tended to reverse word sequences. They read words backwards (e.g., was vs saw). This learner group misperceived letters as if seeing them in a mirror (b for d; p for q). Other studies show this learner group taking foreign language classes experienced troubles in both native and foreign languages in processing auditory information from listening, in processing graphic information from print, and using memory from knowledge and information from thoughts for speaking in both native and foreign languages (Sparks, 1995; Sparks & Ganschow, 1993, 1995; Sparks, Ganschow, Javorsky, Pohlman, & Patton, 1992; Sparks, Ganschow, Kenneweg, & Miller, 1991; Sparks, Ganschow, & Pohlman, 1989; DeFino & Lombardino, 2004; Barrera, 2003; Ganschow et al., 1998; DeFino & Lombardino, 2004; Sparks et al., 2006; Sparks et al., 2008). Mabbott (1994) added that learners with learning disabilities experienced similar problems in reading comprehension, oral reading errors, and written errors in native languages and foreign languages such as Spanish, French, and German.

Vellutino and Scanlon (1986) coined the term "linguistic coding" to account for learners with learning disabilities being poor coders and processors of language. Sparks' studies showed that transfer of language processing difficulties from native to second languages occurred. Sparks proposed the Linguistic Coding Deficient Hypothesis (LCDH) as an explanatory model for the transfer of learning disabilities from learners' native languages to foreign languages (Sparks, 1995). More specifically, LCDH posits that native language processing problems carry over

CHAPTER 4

to foreign language processing problems in the areas of phonology, syntax, and semantics (Sparks, 1995; Sparks & Ganschow, 1993, 1995; Sparks, Ganschow, Javorsky, Pohlman, & Patton, 1992; Sparks, Ganschow, Kenneweg, & Miller, 1991; Sparks, Ganschow, & Pohlman, 1989; Sparks et al., 2006; Sparks et al., 2008).

The question is whether learning difficulties of these learners in foreign language classes were due to their learning disabilities. Ganschow et al. (1998) found that the difficulties were due to linguistic coding (Ganschow et al., 1998; Ganschow et al., 2000). Ganschow et al. (2000) studied learners who were statistically more at risk for failing academically than other learners. Some at-risk learners had learning disabilities, while others did not. Ganschow et al. (2000) found that at-risk learners without learning disabilities were similar to at-risk learners with learning disabilities in all tests. Sparks et al. (1992) compared test results between learners identified as high failure risks, low failure risks, and learners with learning disabilities in high school foreign language classes. The tests used were the *Modern Language Aptitude Test* (MLAT), *Wide Range Achievement Test-Revised* (WRAT-R), and the *Woodcock-Johnson Psychoeducational Battery* (WJPEB). They found that the test results for low-risk learners were different from those of learners at high risk. These same low-risk learners also had different test results than did students with learning disabilities. Also, the test results of the high-risk learners were similar to those of learners with learning disabilities in the MLAT, WRAT-R, and WJPEB subtests that covered phonology and syntax. Sparks et al. (1999) found that some, but not all, learners with learning disabilities had foreign language difficulties. Some learners without learning disabilities also experienced foreign language difficulties. The performance of learners with learning disabilities with foreign language difficulties was similar to that of learners without learning disabilities and who had poor foreign language learning skills in terms of IQ, academic achievement, foreign language aptitude, and foreign language course performance outcomes (grade and proficiency). According to Sparks (2006, 2009), no such thing as a disability for learning a foreign language exists as in a "Foreign Language Learning Disability" (FLLD). Learners with learning disabilities performed similarly to poor readers because both groups were poor language learners in general. In addition, Sparks, Ganschow, and colleagues looked into learners' with learning disabilities difficulties with foreign languages based on cognitive, affective, and linguistic explanations, and found that the difficulties were not due to aptitude, motivation, anxiety, attitude, or cognitive abilities (Sparks, Ganschow, & Patton, 2008; Ganschow et al., 1998; Ganschow et al., 2000). They found that the difficulties were due to problematic language processing rather than learner learning disability per se.

Studies of learners with learning disabilities in foreign language classes presumed uniformity among the learners used in processing foreign languages, and found that the learning strategies used were not conducive for foreign language learning. At issue is whether learners with learning disabilities varied in the way they process foreign languages and whether their processing of spoken languages shapes their foreign language learning strategies. Learners with learning disabilities may process language in ways that delimit the learning strategies they adopt. In addition, poor readers within the general education learner population may process language in ways that delimit their strategies for learning how to read. Reading is an auditory encoding process and learners with and without learning disabilities may experience auditory encoding difficulties that affect their reading ability. The issue is whether learning disabilities per se, or disabilities that revolve around sensory-based encoding process shape how learners learn languages, both spoken and signed. Past studies of learners with learning disabilities and general education learners who were poor readers showed that both groups experienced difficulties in learning second languages. These groups experienced difficulties in the auditory encoding process. These difficulties carried over from their spoken first languages to their spoken second languages, and that, therefore, it was the encoding process rather than learning disabilities that affected their ability to process language.

When learners with learning disabilities are introduced to ASL, they are presented with a visual language that uses a different modality than do spoken foreign languages. This brings into inquiry on whether they differ in their language processing of and strategies for learning a foreign signed language such as ASL. The question now is whether encoding difficulties learners experience in learning auditory-based languages carry over to the learning of visually-based signed languages. Another, related, question is if both learners with and without learning disabilities activate alternative language processing schemas in their learning of signed language as a second language. To ascertain this, questionnaire item responses and course performances of learners with and without learning disabilities will be compared for similarities and differences in the processing of and strategies used for learning ASL.

American Sign Language (ASL) presents perceptual and learning issues for learners with learning disabilities. No study on L2 high school learners with and without learning disabilities in ASL classrooms relating to their perception and learning strategy existed before this one, unfortunately. What remains is a discussion of learning strategy and the role language perceptual processing schemas play in determining learners' preferred language learning strategies.

Another issue in second language studies for learners with learning disabilities is their strategies for learning a second language. It is understood in research literature that learners with learning disabilities have developed certain language processing schema and devised particular strategies for learning second languages. The remaining issue is whether there is a relationship between language processing and learning strategy for high school learners with learning disabilities who learn ASL as a foreign language.

Since this study looks at how the preferred language processing schemas of learners' with learning disabilities shape their learning strategies, the language processing schemas used must be statistically analyzed first, followed by assignment of learners to various cluster memberships, and then comparisons will be made regarding the preferred language learning strategies used across clusters.

Method for Ascertaining Learners' Preferred Language Perceptual Processing Schemas and Language Learning Strategies

The questionnaire, in Appendix B, included items regarding learners' preferred language perceptual processing schemas and language learning strategies. In order to obtain this information, a part of the questionnaire, entitled "Learning and Using ASL," was prepared. The subpart about language perceptual processing schema contained three items. These items were built on study findings by Barbe and Swassing

LEARNING ASL AS A FOREIGN LANGUAGE

(1979), Dunn and Dunn (1983), and Peterson's *Beliefs about Learning American Sign Language*. The questionnaire asked, "When I learn new signs (including vocabulary and sentences), how do I think?" The three answer choices given are "I think of pictures and images that describe the new signs., " "I think of actions that describe the new signs," and "I think of its English translation."

The part on learning strategies contained 24 items. The language learning strategies in the questionnaire identified from the research literature include metacognitive, cognitive, linguistic, social, and affective components. The LLS items and related components appearing in the questionnaire included thinking strategy (cognitive), note-taking strategy (metacognitive), reliance on L1 languages (linguistic), preferred language for learning ASL (social), learning activities (social and affective), questioning sources (affective), and preferred linguistic area of study in ASL used to learn it. The constructs for learning strategy items included in the questionnaire were drawn from several sources including Oxford's *SILL*, Horwitz's *BALLI*, and Peterson's *Beliefs about Learning American Sign Language*. The items concerning thinking strategies were part of the language perceptual processing schema described in the previous paragraph. The interest here was on learners' reliance on L1 languages when learning ASL, their preferred linguistic area of study when learning ASL, note-taking strategies, learning activities, and sources for answers to their questions. Oxford's *SILL* provided constructs for social strategies used, including interaction with teachers and learners, and for cognitive strategies used, including note-taking. The constructs involved with reliance on L1 languages and linguistic levels for learning ASL were derived from *BALLI*'s section on "The Nature of Language Learning." Horwitz discussed learners' beliefs that learning another language involved translating from English to another language, as well as learning vocabulary and grammar. The communication-centered learning construct in *BALLI* influenced the questions about the type of language discourse used.

The different learning activities selected for this study as part of LLSs have sensory processing requirements. Learning activities exist in print form and others in differing visual formats. The print media included textbooks, homework, projects, and games. The other visually-related learning activities included narration, dialogues, homework, projects, watching class lessons, doing grammar exercises, and playing games. Textbooks, homework, and projects relate to both sensory processing qualities. These learning activities containing different sensory processing qualities were presented to learner respondents, and their responses to these questions will help in our assessment of whether the association between their preferred sensory media used in language learning activities was similar or not to their preferred language perceptual processing schema.

Each LLS area was expressed in question format and different learning strategies within each LLS area became answer choices. For example, the question, "How do I take notes of new signs to help me remember them?" the given answer choices were "I draw pictures and images that describe new signs," "I put down actions that describe the new signs," and "I put down English words for new ASL signs." Other questions posed and related answer choices can be seen in the questionnaire in Appendix B.

Results from the Questions Related to Language Processing Schemas in Processing ASL

Learners without Learning Disabilities

The questionnaire contained items about the perceptual schemas learners used in processing new ASL signs. These processing schemas included thinking in pictures and images, thinking of actions for signs, and thinking of a sign's English translation. Table 9 shows that most learners learned new signs by by thinking of actions that described new signs. Fewer learners thought of pictures and images when learning new signs. The fewest number of learners thought of English translations for new signs they learned.

Table 9. Language Perceptual Processing Schemas of Learners without Learning Disabilities in Answer to the Question: When I Learn New Signs (including vocabulary and sentences), How Do I Think?

Language Perceptual Processing Schemas	Answers	
	Agree	Disagree
I think of pictures and images that describe the new signs.	68.6	31.4
I think of actions that describe the new signs.	90.0	10.0
I think of its English translation.	61.9	38.1

Note: Figures are in percentages.

The next task was to ascertain whether learners varied in their preferred processing schemas by age, gender, and ASL course level groups. Age groups did not significantly differ in preferred processing schemas, with one exception. The learners significantly differed in the thinking in pictures and images strategy. Post-hoc tests shows that 14-year-olds (M = 1.50, SD = .522) significantly differed from 15-year-olds (M = 1.12, SD = .332) at $p = .012$ and 16-year-olds (M = 1.00, SD = .000) at $p = .013$. There were no significant differences between gender groups for all processing schemas.

One significant difference that existed between learners in different ASL level courses was in the strategy of thinking about signs in pictures and images. Post-hoc tests show that on thinking in pictures and images, significant differences existed between ASL Level 1 learners (M = 1.41, SD = .495), Level 2 learners (M = 1.25, SD = .434) at $p = .02$, and Level 3 learners (M = 1.22, SD = .418) at $p = .016$. These numbers show that learners in higher level ASL courses tended to think of new signs in picture and image formats than did learners in lower course levels. No other significant differences in other processing schemas between learners in different ASL course levels were found.

Students of different age, gender, and ASL course level groups were largely similar to each other in almost all language processing variables. The next set of analyses for this group will focus on responses of learners of different ages, genders, and ASL course levels to learning strategy-related questions and about course performance grades.

Learners with Learning Disabilities

The main issue for learners with learning disabilities learning foreign languages is their language processing skills. These learners' responses to questionnaire items about language perceptual processing schemas were used to create learner clusters based on their preferred processing schemas for learning new signs in response to foreign language literature about the sensory processing of languages. The learner clusters included learners who thought of new signs as pictures and images, those who thought in terms of actions, and those who thought of English translation of signs.

The Thinking in Pictures and Images and Thinking in English Translations were the two functions that significantly differentiated learners into language perceptual processing groups. The Thinking in Pictures

Chapter 4

and Images variable covered about 73% of the learners and the Thinking in English Translations variable covered about 27% of the learners. The thinking in actions variable did not differentiate learners; all learners preferred thinking in actions when learning new ASL signs. This variable is included in each of the learners' preferred perceptual processing schemas. The next task was to find whether learners with learning disabilities differed in thinking strategy by age, gender, and ASL course level groups. Information about age and gender was for the two schools and that of the course level group was for the other school.

It is found that, with one exception, the relationship between gender and thinking in English translation is not significant ($F[1] = 4.659, p < .05$). The sole exception was that females to a greater extent than males tended to think of English translations when processing ASL signs. There were also no significant differences among learners from different age groups and ASL course levels in their perceptual processing schemas for ASL.

In general, it was clear from the data obtained that, with a few exceptions, learners with learning disabilities did not significantly differ from each other in their preferred perceptual schemas for processing ASL by age, gender, and ASL course level. Likewise for learners without disabilities, the variables of age, gender, and ASL course level groups were eliminated from further analysis. The next step was to seek relationships between age, gender, and ASL course levels and learning strategies; and course performance for all learners with learning disabilities.

Comparison in Language Processing between General Education Learners and Learners with Learning Disabilities

To ascertain whether language processing differences existed between general education learners and learners with learning disabilities, the two groups' questionnaire answers were compared. Most of the general education learners thought in actions, while a little more than half of them thought in pictures, images, and in English translations of signs. Learners with learning disabilities largely thought mainly in pictures, images, and actions, while a little more than half thought in terms of English translations for signs. The two groups' thinking strategies did not differ by age, gender, or ASL course level.

Learning ASL as a Foreign Language

Learner Learning Strategies
General Education Learners

These learners were asked about their use of several learning strategies. Table 10 shows results for each answer item under different learning strategies. The table shows many similarities between learners. A few differences can be discerned in learner learning strategies, however. All numbers given here are in percentages and reflect the number of learners employing the same learning strategy.

Students differed in their preferences for taking notes in pictures and images or by putting down actions to help them learn ASL in their wanting to have only spoken English or only ASL used in class; wanting to learn ASL by giving narratives using other sources such as textbooks dictionaries, and/or the Internet to help them learn ASL and in emphasizing discourse when learning ASL. The interest here was to find out if learners in different age groups, genders, and taking different level ASL courses learn ASL differently. Table 11 shows results for language learning strategies preferred by learners in different age groups, with levels of significance.

The table shows that there were no significant differences among age groups in its learners' preferences for doing narratives, watching classroom activities as a learning activity, and translating from English to ASL and vice versa. It does show a few significant differences among age groups in the use of some language learning strategies. Older learners relied on English sentences; tended not to prefer that their teachers use spoken English in class; preferred to learn ASL by playing ASL games; and emphasized the learning of ASL grammar and discourse rules more so than did the younger learners. Younger learners preferred doing homework to learn ASL more so than older learners.

Table 12 shows results for language learning strategies preferred by learners of different genders with levels of significance. The table showed a few significant differences between gender groups in some language learning strategies. From the table data, it can be discerned that female learners, more than males, tended to put down actions describing new signs, preferred to do dialogues and play language games when learning ASL, asked their teachers if they have questions, and emphasized the

Chapter 4

Table 10. Learning Strategies Preferred by General Education Learners.

Learning Strategies	Answers	
	Agree	Disagree
How much does my first language, such as English, influence my learning of ASL?		
I think of English words when I learn new ASL signs.	90.4	9.6
I think of English sentences when I learn new ASL sentences.	73.2	26.8
How do I take notes of new signs to help me remember them?		
I draw pictures and images that describe new signs.	21.5	78.5
I put down actions that describes the new signs.	47.4	52.6
I put down English words for new ASL signs.	77.6	22.4
During American Sign Language class, I would like:		
To have a combination of ASL and English spoken.	79.5	20.5
To have as much English as possible spoken.	20.0	80.0
To have only ASL signed.	34.8	65.2
I learn better when:		
I give narrations	45.4	54.6
I do dialogues with other people in class	82.3	17.7
I follow the learner textbook	12.9	87.1
I listen (watch) activities	90.5	9.5
I do grammar exercises	50.0	50.0
I play ASL games in class	75.7	24.3
I do homework	57.9	42.1
I do project work	56.3	46.4
I translate from English to ASL	78.9	21.1
I translate from ASL to English	88.0	12.0
Whenever I don't know signs:		
I ask the teacher.	92.9	7.1
I ask other learners.	90.0	10.0
I look up in the textbook dictionary, Internet, CDs, or videos.	48.8	51.2
When I learn ASL:		
I emphasize vocabulary.	86.2	13.8
I emphasize grammar.	61.0	39.0
I emphasize discourse.	41.1	58.9

Note: Figures are in percentages.

Table 11. ANOVA Results for Language Learning Strategies by Age of General Education Learners.

Language Learning Strategies	Age Groups						p
	13	14	15	16	17	18	
How much does my first language, such as English, influence my learning of ASL?							
I think of English words when I learn new ASL signs.	1.14	1.11	1.09	1.06	1.13	1.00	.909
I think of English sentences when I learn new ASL sentences.	1.14	1.17	1.19	1.23	1.66	1.33	.000
How do I take notes of new signs to help me remember them?							
I draw pictures and images that describe new signs.	1.86	1.83	1.71	1.81	1.79	1.67	.724
I put down actions that describes the new signs.	1.58	1.54	1.59	1.51	1.36	2.00	.205
I put down English words for new ASL signs.	1.42	1.17	1.18	1.23	1.40	1.33	.179
During American Sign Language class, I would like:							
To have a combination of ASL and English spoken.	1.14	1.17	1.19	1.23	1.66	1.33	.507
To have as much English as possible spoken.	1.71	1.68	1.86	1.79	1.97	1.67	.019
To have only ASL signed.	1.86	1.75	1.53	1.70	1.58	1.67	.105
I learn better when:							
I give narrations	1.57	1.62	1.51	1.44	1.63	1.67	.458
I do dialogues with other people in class	1.00	1.27	1.12	1.17	1.15	1.00	.210
I follow the learners' textbook	1.86	1.79	1.93	1.85	1.94	2.00	.214
I listen (watch) activities	1.00	1.14	1.07	1.11	1.06	1.00	.607
I do grammar exercises	1.57	1.56	1.56	1.36	1.48	1.33	.337
I play ASL games in class	1.57	1.43	1.14	1.15	1.15	1.00	.000

(*Continues*)

Table 11. (*Continued*)

Language Learning Strategies	Age Groups						*p*
	13	14	15	16	17	18	
I do homework	1.28	1.26	1.51	1.49	1.48	1.67	.045
I do project work	1.43	1.56	1.53	1.34	1.33	1.67	.105
I translate from English to ASL	1.29	1.21	1.23	1.17	1.24	1.00	.879
I translate from ASL to English	1.14	1.11	1.14	1.15	1.06	1.00	.829
Whenever I don't know signs:							
I ask the teacher.	1.00	1.14	1.05	1.06	1.00	1.00	.131
I ask other learners.	1.00	1.16	1.11	1.04	1.09	1.00	.386
I look up in the textbook dictionary, Internet, CDs, or videos.	1.57	1.61	1.51	1.47	1.36	1.67	.293
When I learn ASL:							
I emphasize vocabulary.	1.29	1.16	1.18	1.11	1.06	1.00	.458
I emphasize grammar.	1.71	1.51	1.40	1.28	1.27	1.00	.021
I emphasize discourse.	1.86	1.60	1.60	1.67	1.42	1.00	.041

Table 12. ANOVA Results for Language Learning Strategies by Gender of General Education Learners.

Language Learning Strategies	Gender		p
	Males	Females	
How much does my first language, such as English, influence my learning of ASL?			
I think of English words when I learn new ASL signs.	1.11	1.09	.561
I think of English sentences when I learn new ASL sentences.	1.23	1.29	.344
How do I take notes of new signs to help me remember them?			
I draw pictures and images that describe new signs.	1.82	1.77	.402
I put down actions that describes the new signs.	1.63	1.46	.017
I put down English words for new ASL signs.	1.18	1.25	.257
During American Sign Language class, I would like:			
To have a combination of ASL and English spoken.	1.17	1.23	.330
To have as much English as possible spoken.	1.62	1.91	.000
To have only ASL signed.	1.71	1.62	.183
I learn better when:			
I give narrations	1.58	1.52	.416
I do dialogues with other people in class	1.24	1.13	.042
I follow the learners' textbook	1.83	1.90	.145
I listen (watch) activities	1.22	1.08	.293
I do grammar exercises	1.46	1.52	.398
I play ASL games in class	1.33	1.19	.019
I do homework	1.38	1.45	.374
I do project work	1.53	1.42	.125
I translate from English to ASL	1.19	1.23	.477
I translate from ASL to English	1.16	1.09	.149
Whenever I don't know signs:			
I ask the teacher.	1.12	1.04	.023
I ask other learners.	1.13	1.08	.188
I look up in the textbook dictionary, Internet, CDs, or videos.	1.52	1.50	.774
When I learn ASL:			
I emphasize vocabulary.	1.21	1.09	.020
I emphasize grammar.	1.49	1.33	.021
I emphasize discourse.	1.61	1.5	.593

learning of both vocabulary and grammar. Male learners, to a greater extent than females, preferred to have spoken English used in their classes as much as possible.

The next area of analysis was to assess whether learners in different ASL course levels differed in their preferred language learning strategies. Descriptive analysis was conducted to obtain group means and ANOVA statistics were performed to ascertain if any significant differences could be seen in these groups. Table 13 shows results for language learning strategies preferred by learners taking different level ASL courses, with levels of significance.

As seen in table 14, learners taking lower level ASL courses tended to think more in English sentences when learning new ASL signs than did learners taking higher level ASL courses. No significant differences occurred between learners taking different ASL course levels in learners' preferences for taking notes in pictures and images and in actions. Learners in lower ASL course levels tended to write down English words for new ASL signs more so than did learners in the highest level ASL course.

Significant differences existed among some learners in differing ASL course levels in their preferences as to which language should be used in ASL classroom communication. Learners in lower level ASL courses preferred that a combination of ASL and English be used in their classrooms than did learners in the highest level ASL course. Learners in lower level ASL courses also tended to prefer that only spoken English be used in their classrooms than did learners in the highest level ASL course. No significant differences were seen between learners in different ASL course levels for learners' preference that only ASL be used for communication in their classrooms.

Regarding learners' preferred language learning activities, learners taking different level ASL courses differed significantly from others in several activities. Learners in Level 1 courses preferred to learn ASL by watching classroom activities than did those in Level 2 courses. Learners in lower level ASL courses preferred learning from textbooks than did learners in higher level ASL courses. Learners taking higher level ASL courses preferred learning by playing ASL games in class than did learners taking the lowest level ASL course. Students in lower level ASL courses much preferred doing homework than did learners in higher level courses.

Learning ASL as a Foreign Language

Table 13. ANOVA Results for Language Learning Strategies
by ASL Course Level of General Education Learners.

Language Learning Strategies	ASL Course Level 1	2	3	p
How much does my first language, such as English, influence my learning of ASL?				
I think of English words when I learn new ASL signs.	1.19	1.06	1.10	.493
I think of English sentences when I learn new ASL sentences.	1.19	1.22	1.48	.000
How do I take notes of new signs to help me remember them?				
I draw pictures and images that describe new signs.	1.79	1.78	1.78	.995
I put down actions that describes the new signs.	1.51	1.51	1.58	.687
I put down English words for new ASL signs.	1.18	1.18	1.36	.030
During American Sign Language class, I would like:				
To have a combination of ASL and English spoken.	1.12	1.23	1.34	.006
To have as much English as possible spoken.	1.68	1.86	1.94	.000
To have only ASL signed.	1.72	1.62	1.56	.120
I learn better when:				
I give narrations	1.60	1.55	1.45	.242
I do dialogues with other people in class	1.25	1.11	1.14	.052
I follow the learners' textbook	1.80	1.94	1.92	.015
I listen (watch) activities	1.15	1.03	1.08	.038
I do grammar exercises	1.52	1.52	1.44	.625
I play ASL games in class	1.42	1.09	1.12	.000
I do homework	1.31	1.44	1.60	.003
I do project work	1.57	1.42	1.32	.012
I translate from English to ASL	1.22	1.18	1.24	.744
I translate from ASL to English	1.13	1.15	1.06	.304
Whenever I don't know signs:				
I ask the teacher.	1.12	1.06	1.00	.031
I ask other learners.	1.18	1.05	1.02	.002
I look up in the textbook dictionary, Internet, CDs, or videos.	1.61	1.59	1.22	.000
When I learn ASL:				
I emphasize vocabulary.	1.18	1.14	1.06	.136
I emphasize grammar.	1.49	1.38	1.22	.006
I emphasize discourse.	1.65	1.52	1.56	.242

Chapter 4

Learners in lower level ASL courses also preferred doing class projects than did learners in higher level courses.

Learners taking the highest level ASL courses tended to ask questions of their teachers more often than did learners in the lowest level ASL courses. Learners taking higher level ASL courses also tended to ask questions of other learners more than did learners in the lowest level ASL courses. Learners taking the highest level ASL courses preferred looking information up in textbooks, dictionaries, the Internet, or on CDs or videos for answers to their questions than did learners in lower level ASL courses.

No significant differences existed between learners in different ASL course levels in their preference for learning ASL vocabulary and discourse. The data in table 13, however, suggests that learners in higher level ASL courses emphasized the learning of ASL grammar more so than did learners in the lowest level ASL courses.

Learners with Learning Disabilities

Respondents with learning disabilities were asked about their preferred strategies for learning ASL. Table 14 shows results for each answer item under different learning strategies.

Learners with learning disabilities largely preferred learning ASL by writing actions and English words in their notes; using both ASL and English when learning ASL; using English words and sentences as aids in using and remembering ASL signs; doing paired dialogues; listening and watching teachers and other learners do the same; doing grammar exercises; playing language games; and by doing homework, class, and research projects. They also said they learned ASL best by translating from English to ASL and vice versa; they asked teachers and other learners for assistance; and they emphasized vocabulary in their learning of ASL.

These learners did not prefer taking notes in pictures and images; using only English or only ASL in the classroom; learning ASL by giving narratives; or using textbooks, dictionaries, and the Internet to assist them. They did not think that grammar and discourse should be emphasized when learning ASL.

Table 15 depicts results for the relationship between learners' ages and their preferred language learning strategies. Table 15 shows no

LEARNING ASL AS A FOREIGN LANGUAGE

Table 14. Learning Strategies Used by Learners with Learning Disabilities.

Learning Strategies	Answers	
	Agree	Disagree
How much does my first language, such as English, influence my learning of ASL?		
I think of English words when I learn new ASL signs.	81.6	18.4
I think of English sentences when I learn new ASL sentences.	57.9	42.1
How do I take notes of new signs to help me remember them?		
I draw pictures and images that describe new signs.	24.3	75.7
I put down actions that describes the new signs.	52.6	47.4
I put down English words for new ASL signs.	65.8	34.2
During American Sign Language class, I would like:		
To have a combination of ASL and English spoken.	76.3	23.7
To have as much English as possible spoken.	7.9	92.1
To have only ASL signed.	23.7	76.3
I learn better when:		
I give narrations	39.5	60.5
I do dialogues with other people in class	64.9	35.1
I follow the learners' textbook	34.2	65.8
I listen (watch) activities	89.5	10.5
I do grammar exercises	71.1	28.9
I play ASL games in class	97.4	2.6
I do homework	73.7	26.3
I do project work	73.0	27.0
I translate from English to ASL	65.8	34.2
I translate from ASL to English	84.2	15.8
Whenever I don't know signs:		
I ask the teacher.	100.0	0.0
I ask other learners.	94.6	5.4
I look up in the textbook dictionary, Internet, CDs, or videos.	43.2	56.8
When I learn ASL:		
I emphasize vocabulary.	73.7	26.3
I emphasize grammar.	47.4	52.6
I emphasize discourse.	47.4	52.6

Note: Figures are in percentages.

Chapter 4

Table 15. ANOVA Results for Language Learning Strategies by Age for Learners with Learning Disabilities.

Language Learning Strategies	Age Groups				p
	14	15	16	17	
How much does my first language, such as English, influence my learning of ASL?					
I think of English words when I learn new ASL signs.	1.33	1.06	1.17	1.50	.200
I think of English sentences when I learn new ASL sentences.	1.67	1.29	1.33	1.50	.249
How do I take notes of new signs to help me remember them?					
I draw pictures and images that describe new signs.	1.92	1.59	1.80	2.00	.192
I put down actions that describe the new signs.	1.42	1.59	1.33	1.50	.708
I put down English words for new ASL signs.	1.08	1.35	1.67	1.50	.081
During American Sign Language class, I would like:					
To have a combination of ASL and English spoken.	1.17	1.18	1.33	1.50	.650
To have as much English as possible spoken.	1.92	1.88	2.00	2.00	.819
To have only ASL signed.	1.83	1.82	1.67	1.00	.062
I learn better when:					
I give narrations	1.67	1.65	1.67	1.00	.345
I do dialogues with other people in class	1.50	1.25	1.50	1.00	.346
I follow the learners' textbook	1.92	1.41	1.83	1.50	.024
I listen (watch) activities	1.08	1.12	1.17	1.00	.919
I do grammar exercises	1.50	1.18	1.17	1.00	.179
I play ASL games in class	1.00	1.00	1.00	1.50	.000
I do homework	1.08	1.29	1.50	1.00	.208
I do project work	1.25	1.25	1.33	1.00	.847
I translate from English to ASL	1.50	1.24	1.33	1.50	.528
I translate from ASL to English	1.17	1.06	1.33	1.00	.375
Whenever I don't know signs:					
I ask the teacher.	1.00	1.00	1.00	1.00	1.00
I ask other learners.	1.00	1.06	1.17	1.00	.566
I look up in the textbook dictionary, Internet, CDs, or videos.	1.17	1.59	1.33	1.00	.400
When I learn ASL:					
I emphasize vocabulary.	1.33	1.24	1.33	1.00	.774
I emphasize grammar.	1.67	1.47	1.50	1.00	.362
I emphasize discourse.	1.42	1.65	1.50	1.00	.307

significant differences in learning strategies used between learners with learning disabilities of different age groups, except for two. Learners significantly differed in their preferences for learning ASL from textbooks and by playing ASL games. Older learners tended to prefer learning ASL from textbooks than did younger learners. Younger learners, by contrast, preferred learning ASL by playing ASL games.

Table 16 shows language learning strategy preferences by learners of different genders, with levels of significance. As depicted in the table, female learners preferred relying on L1 English sentences for learning ASL grammar and for learning ASL by watching classroom activities than did male learners. No significant differences existed between male and female learners in other learning strategies used.

Table 17 shows that learners taking different level ASL courses significantly differed in their preference for learning ASL from textbooks. Descriptive statistics demonstrated that learners taking lower level ASL courses preferred to learn ASL from textbooks than did learners in higher level ASL courses. Learners taking different level ASL courses did not differ in their preferences for the other learning strategies.

Comparison of Learning Strategies between General Education Learners and Learners with Learning Disabilities

To ascertain if differences existed between general education learners and learners with learning disabilities, their responses to questionnaire items on thinking and learning strategies were compared. Most learners in both groups used many of the same learning strategies for learning ASL. Learners in both groups taking lower level ASL courses preferred learning ASL from textbooks.

Both groups of learners differed in some preferences for learning ASL. Learners with learning disabilities preferred to write actions down to help them learn ASL signs, they used English words and sentences to understand ASL, and preferred to learn vocabulary. General education learners emphasized that learning grammar, as well as vocabulary, was also important.

Both groups of learners also differed in the use of some learning strategies by age and gender. Younger learners with learning disabilities

Table 16. ANOVA Results for Language Learning Strategies by Gender for Learners with Learning Disabilities.

Language Learning Strategies	Gender		p
	Males	Females	
How much does my first language, such as English, influence my learning of ASL?			
I think of English words when I learn new ASL signs.	1.18	1.19	.915
I think of English sentences when I learn new ASL sentences.	1.65	1.24	.010
How do I take notes of new signs to help me remember them?			
I draw pictures and images that describe new signs.	1.75	1.76	.936
I put down actions that describes the new signs.	1.35	1.57	.189
I put down English words for new ASL signs.	1.29	1.38	.587
During American Sign Language class, I would like:			
To have a combination of ASL and English spoken.	1.24	1.24	.984
To have as much English as possible spoken.	1.88	1.95	.440
To have only ASL signed.	1.82	1.71	.445
I learn better when:			
I give narrations	1.71	1.52	.266
I do dialogues with other people in class	1.38	1.33	.799
I follow the learners' textbook	1.53	1.76	.140
I listen (watch) activities	1.24	1.00	.018
I do grammar exercises	1.35	1.24	.451
I play ASL games in class	1.00	1.05	.375
I do homework	1.18	1.33	.287
I do project work	1.38	1.19	.222
I translate from English to ASL	1.35	1.33	.903
I translate from ASL to English	1.12	1.19	.553
Whenever I don't know signs:			
I ask the teacher.	1.00	1.00	1.00
I ask other learners.	1.00	1.10	.190
I look up in the textbook dictionary, Internet, CDs, or videos.	1.53	1.60	.676
When I learn ASL:			
I emphasize vocabulary.	1.35	1.19	.270
I emphasize grammar.	1.35	1.67	.056
I emphasize discourse.	1.65	1.43	.189

Table 17. ANOVA Results for Language Learning Strategies by ASL Course Level for Learners with Learning Disabilities.

Language Learning Strategies	ASL Course Level			p
	1	2	3	
How much does my first language, such as English, influence my learning of ASL?				
I think of English words when I learn new ASL signs.	1.00	1.20	2.00	.056
I think of English sentences when I learn new ASL sentences.	1.29	1.20	2.00	.336
How do I take notes of new signs to help me remember them?				
I draw pictures and images that describe new signs.	1.65	2.00	2.00	.115
I put down actions that describes the new signs.	1.50	1.60	1.00	.878
I put down English words for new ASL signs.	1.36	1.60	2.00	.252
During American Sign Language class, I would like:				
To have a combination of ASL and English spoken.	1.29	1.40	1.00	.761
To have as much English as possible spoken.	1.86	2.00	2.00	.731
To have only ASL signed.	1.79	1.60	1.00	.333
I learn better when:				
I give narrations	1.71	1.40	1.00	.536
I do dialogues with other people in class	1.46	1.20	1.00	.638
I follow the learners' textbook	1.36	1.80	1.00	.010
I listen (watch) activities	1.14	1.20	1.00	.789
I do grammar exercises	1.21	1.20	1.00	.068
I play ASL games in class	1.00	1.20	1.00	.154
I do homework	1.43	1.20	1.00	.498
I do project work	1.23	1.40	1.00	.522
I translate from English to ASL	1.29	1.20	2.00	.059
I translate from ASL to English	1.07	1.20	1.00	.548
Whenever I don't know signs:				
I ask the teacher.	1.00	1.00	1.00	1.00
I ask other learners.	1.07	1.25	1.00	.414
I look up in the textbook dictionary, Internet, CDs, or videos.	1.57	1.25	1.00	.359
When I learn ASL:				
I emphasize vocabulary.	1.14	1.40	1.00	.513
I emphasize grammar.	1.50	1.40	1.00	.437
I emphasize discourse.	1.64	1.40	1.00	.402

preferred learning ASL from textbooks while younger general education learners did not. Differences existed between gender groups of general education learners as previously discussed, while there were no differences among gender groups of learners with learning disabilities in learning strategies used.

Motivation and Language Processing Predictors of Language Learning Strategies

General Education Learners

While general education learners of different ages, genders, and in different level ASL courses significantly differed from each other in using a few learning strategies, it still needs to be determined if their preferred learning strategies were predicted by their motivation and preferred language perceptual processing schemas regardless of their ages, genders, and ASL course levels. Motivation and perceptual processing schema may have contributed to learners' preferred learning strategies whereby learners performed activities to encode the linguistic and extra-linguistic features of the language. They did this while learning about the language, community, and culture of signing D/HH people in ways that were similar to their reasons for taking ASL and the way they processed ASL as a language.

To identify possible motivation and language perceptual processing predictors of learners' learning strategy, a linear regression analysis was employed. Linear regression is a statistic that, in this study, adds correlations among motivation and language perceptual processing variables in a stepwise fashion to create a cumulative effect on learning strategies. It is used to find combinations of independent variables that are highly intercorrelated and predict results of a dependent variable. It is possible that there may be no independent variables that highly predict results of the dependent variable.

The motivation and language perceptual processing variables were the predictors and independent variables, and learning strategy was the dependent variable. Results of the linear regression analysis will inform us which motivation and language perceptual processing variables were predictors of learners' learning strategies. It will tell us about the direction among the predictors for predicting learners' strategies in learning the language. The results are reported by learning strategies used.

Some regressions began with motivation variables and compounded with language perceptual processing variables to predict learning strategies, and other regressions began with language perceptual processing variables and compounded with motivation variables to predict learning strategies. Some of the learning strategies were predicted by only motivation predictors, and other strategies by only language perceptual processing predictors. Note-taking in English words and learning by listening (watching) were the two learning strategies to have no predictors. To ensure that motivation and perception variables were significant predictors for each of the learning strategies, p values were calculated. The regression is significant if the p is 0.05 or less. Tables 17–22 present significant motivation and/or language perceptual processing predictors for the different learning strategies. Results are discussed in the order of motivation and language perceptual processing predictors of learning strategies. Correlation scores were also given to demonstrate the strength of the linear relationships between motivation and language perceptual processing predictors of learning strategies.

Results are discussed regarding motivation and language perceptual processing predictors of learning strategies that related to reliance on L1 languages, preferred language for learning ASL, preferred linguistic area of study in ASL used to learn the language, preferred note-taking methods, preferred learning activities, and preferred methods learners used to obtain answers to their questions. Correlation coefficients were also provided to demonstrate the strength of the relationship between predictors and learning strategies. The 'r' figures in parentheses indicate the strength of the correlations.

Reliance on L1 English to Learn ASL

Table 18 shows learners' reliance on their L1 language, English, to process ASL signs and sentences. When learning new signs and sentences, learners who thought of English translations were predicted to rely on L1 English words to process ASL signs ($r = .241$). In addition, learners who took ASL because they thought it would be easy to learn,

Table 18. Results of the Regression Analysis of Motivation and Language Perceptual Processing as Independent Variables and Reliance on L1 English for Learning ASL as Dependent Variable for General Education Learners.

Predictors		Dependent Variable		Final Model		
Motivation	Perception	Learning Strategy		B	SE[a] B	Beta
		Reliance on L1 English for Learning ASL				
	ThinkEngTransl			.145	.041	.241***
		FrmL1EngWord				
R^2			.058			
F for change in R^2			12.507			
	ThinkEngTransl			.288	.060	.315***
TakeEasyLearn				.070	.027	.171**
		FromL1EngSent				
R^2			.121			
F for change in R^2			6.732			

Notes: B stands for regression coefficient.
***$p < .001$; **$p < .01$; *$p < .05$.
[a]The "SE" for linear regression in its Final Model refers to how sample results vary from (i.e., covary with) the line of regression. The higher the SE, the more distant a sample is from the line of regression. Conversely, the lower the SE, the closer a sample is to the line of regression.

and who thought of English translations of signs while learning new ASL sentences, were predicted to rely on L1 English sentences when processing new ASL sentences (r = .348).

Preferred Classroom Language for Learning ASL

The following Table 19 shows learners' preferred classroom language for learning ASL. When learning new signs, learners who thought of English translations for signs were predicted to prefer both ASL and English be used as the language of communication in classrooms when learning ASL (r = .176). Learners motivated to take ASL because of a need to communicate with family members, but did not have intellectual interest in the language, were predicted to prefer that only English be used as the ASL classroom communication language (r = .398). Learners who did not think of English translations when learning new signs, but took ASL to help improve their English literacy

Table 19. Results of the Regression Analysis of the Motivation and Language Perceptual Processing as Independent Variables and Preferred Classroom Language for Learning ASL as Dependent Variable for General Education Learners.

Predictors		Dependent Variable	Final Model		
Motivation	Perception	Learning Strategy	B	SE B	Beta
		Preferred Classroom Language for Learning ASL			
	ThinkEngTransl		.146	.057	.176*
		LrnWantBothASLEng			
R^2		.031			
F for change in R^2		6.544			
IntellIntLang			−.222	.042	−.342***
TakeCommFam			.099	.032	.197**
		LrnWantOnlyEng			
R^2		.158			
F for change in R^2		9.387			
	ThinkEngTransl		−.154	.068	−.156*
TakeLearnEng			.067	.033	.138*
		LrnWantOnlyASL			
R^2		.039			
F for change in R^2		3.976			

Notes: B stands for regression coefficient.
***$p < .001$; **$p < .01$; *$p < .05$.

skills, were predicted to prefer that only ASL be used as the ASL classroom communication language (r = .197).

Preferred Linguistic Area of Study for Learning ASL

Table 20 below presents learners' preferred linguistic level for learning ASL. Learners motivated to take ASL because they found it unique were predicted to emphasize learning ASL vocabulary (r = .333). Learners motivated to take ASL because they wanted to become ASL teachers, wanted the personal challenge of learning the language, and thought in actions when learning ASL signs, were predicted to emphasize learning ASL grammar (r = .382). Learners motivated to take ASL because of both an intellectual interest in the language and the fact they had not performed well in other (spoken) foreign language classes were predicted to emphasize learning ASL discourse (r = .226).

CHAPTER 4

Table 20. Results of the Regression Analysis of the Motivation and Language Perceptual Processing Schemas as Independent Variables and Preferred Linguistic Area of Study for Learning ASL as Dependent Variable for General Education Learners.

Predictors		Dependent Variable		Final Model		
Motivation	Perception	Learning Strategy		B	SE B	*Beta*
		Preferred Linguistic Area of Study for Learning ASL				
TakeUniqLang				.163	.032	.334***
		LrnEmphVocab				
R^2			.111			
F for change in R^2			25.543			
TakeTeacherASL				.118	.034	.231***
TakeChallMys				.101	.034	.195**
	ThinkActions			.277	.105	.172**
		LrnEmphGramm				
R^2			.146			
F for change in R^2			6.940			
IntelIntLang				.146	.056	.182**
TakeFailOthLang				.069	.030	.162*
		LrnEmphDiscourse				
R^2			.051			
F for change in R^2			5.390			

Notes: B stands for regression coefficient.
***p < .001; **p < .01; *p < .05.

Note-Taking Strategies

Table 21 presents learners' note-taking strategies. Learners motivated to take ASL because of career plans and thought in pictures and images while learning ASL signs were predicted to put pictures and images of new signs in their class notes (r = .307). Learners motivated to take ASL because of career plans for working with D/HH people, but thought in actions while learning ASL signs, were predicted to put actions representing new signs in their class notes (r = .339). Learners who thought of English translations while learning ASL signs were predicted to write down English words in their class notes (r = .173).

Table 21. Results of the Regression Analysis of the Motivation and Language Perceptual Processing Schemas as Independent Variables and Preferred Note-taking Strategies as Dependent Variable for General Education Learners.

Predictors		Dependent Variable		Final Model		
Motivation	Perception	Learning Strategy		B	SE B	Beta
		Note-taking Strategies				
CareerPlans				.084	.026	.220**
	ThinkPixImag			.153	.060	.174*
		NotePixImag				
R^2			.094			
F for change in R^2			6.444			
CareerPlans				.118	.031	.252***
	ThinkActions			.323	.110	.196**
		NoteActions				
R^2			.115			
F for change in R^2			8.583			
	ThinkEngTransl			.149	.060	.172*
		NoteEngWords				
R^2			.030			
F for change in R^2			6.205			

Notes: B stands for regression coefficient.
***$p < .001$; **$p < .01$; *$p < .05$.

Preferred Learning Activities

Learners' preferred learning activities are presented in table 22. Learners motivated to take ASL because they found it unique and thought of L1 English words while learning new ASL signs were predicted to prefer doing dialogue excercises (r = .212). Learners who were not motivated to take ASL because they wanted to become ASL teachers were predicted to prefer using textbooks (r = .221). Learners motivated to take ASL because of wanting to work with D/HH people were predicted to prefer listening (watching) classroom activities (r = .141). Learners motivated to take ASL because they wanted a personal challenge in learning the language and who thought in actions while learning new signs were predicted to prefer doing grammar exercises (r = .205). Learners motivated to take ASL because they found it unique, but were not interested in learning

Chapter 4

Table 22. Results of the Regression Analysis of the Motivation and Language Perceptual Processing Schemas as Independent Variables and Preferred Learning Activities as Dependent Variable for General Education Learners.

Predictors		Dependent Variable	Final Model		
Motivation	Perception	Learning Strategy	B	SE B	Beta
		Preferred Learning Activities			
TakeUniqLang			.114	.037	.212**
		LrnDoDialogues			
R^2		.045			
F for change in R^2		9.550			
TakeTeacherASL			−.078	.024	−.222***
		LrnFromTextbook			
R^2		.049			
F for change in R^2		10.608			
TakeWorkDeaf			.042	.021	.140*
		LrnByListen(Watch)			
R^2		.020			
F for change in R^2		4.096			
TakeChallMys			.080	.036	.151*
	ThinkActions		.225	.114	.136*
		LrnDoGrammExer			
R^2		.042			
F for change in R^2		3.912			
TakeUniqLang			.200	.048	.332***
TakeLrnDeaf			−.112	.038	−.233**
		LrnByPlayGames			
R^2		.082			
F for change in R^2		8.647			
TakeLearnEng			.075	.035	.150*
		LrnDoHomework			
R^2		.022			
F for change in R^2		4.656			
TakeWorkDeaf			.095	.037	.187*
TakeUniqLang			.122	.051	.174*
TakeCommFam			.085	.041	.136*
			.061	.021	.198**
		LrnDoProject			
R^2		.118			
F for change in R^2		4.174			
	ThinkEngTransl		.212	.057	.251***
		LrnByTransEngASL			
R^2		.063			
F for change in R^2		13.654			

(*Continues*)

Table 22. (*Continued*)

Predictors		Dependent Variable	Final Model		
Motivation	Perception	Learning Strategy	B	SE B	Beta
CareerPlans			.061	.021	.198**
	ThinkEngTransl		.114	.045	.169*
	ThinkActions		.153	.073	.142*
		LrnByTransASLEng			
R^2			.096		
F for change in R^2			4.402		

Notes: B stands for regression coefficient.
***$p < .001$; **$p < .01$; *$p < .05$.

about D/HH people, were predicted to prefer playing ASL learning games in class (r = .286). Learners motivated to take ASL because they needed it for improving English literacy skills were predicted to prefer doing homework (r = .148). Learners motivated to take ASL because they wanted to pursue careers working with D/HH people, found ASL unique, and who took ASL for communication with family members, were predicted to prefer doing class projects (r = .344). Learners who thought of English translations while learning new signs were predicted to prefer translating from English to ASL (r = .251). Learners motivated to take ASL for careers in working with D/HH people and who thought of English translations and actions while learning new signs were predicted to prefer translating from ASL to English (r = .310). There were no motivation or language perceptual processing predictors for doing narratives as an ASL learning strategy.

Learners' Preferred Answer Sources for Questions

Learners' preferred answer sources are shown in Table 23. Learners motivated to take ASL because of intellectual interest in the language were predicted to prefer asking teachers when they did not know signs (r = .253). Learners motivated to take ASL because they found it unique, did not do well in other (spoken) foreign language classes, and did not need to take ASL for communication with friends, were predicted to prefer asking other learners when they did not know signs (r = .319). Learners motivated to

Chapter 4

Table 23. Results of the Regression Analysis of the Motivation and Language Processing Schema as Independent Variables and Preferred Answer Sources for Learner Questions as Dependent Variable for General Education Learners.

Predictors		Dependent Variable		Final Model		
Motivation	Perception	Learning Strategy		B	SE B	Beta
		Preferred Answer Sources for Learner Questions				
IntellIntLang				.106	.028	.253***
		AskTeacher				
R^2			.064			
F for change in R^2			14.003			
TakeUniqLang				.097	.029	.229***
TakeCommFr				−.060	.021	−.199**
TakeFailOthLang				.050	.018	.189**
		AskStudents				
R^2			.102			
F for change in R^2			7.980			
	ThinkActions			.284	.114	.172**
TakeUniqLang				.112	.048	.160*
		AskInternetTxbk				
R^2			.064			
F for change in R^2			5.372			

Notes: B stands for regression coefficient.
***$p < .001$; **$p < .01$; *$p < .05$.

take ASL because they found it unique and who thought in actions when learning ASL signs were predicted to prefer to rely on the Internet, textbooks, and dictionaries when they did not know signs ($r = .253$).

Learners with Learning Disabilities

To find relationships between the two clusters of language perceptual processing functions and learners' preferred language learning strategies, a correlational analysis was warranted. The task was to compare the two clusters of learner responses to the questionnaire items about language learning strategies. Information was solicited from learners about the six learning strategies they used in ASL classrooms. This was done to ascertain the relationship between language perceptual processing schemas and language learning strategies. One-tailed Spearman rho correlation statistic was employed. The results are shown in table 24.

Significant relationships between learners' language perceptual processing schemas and their preferred language learning strategies were determined. The function of learners thinking in pictures and images significantly correlated with the note-taking strategy of drawing pictures and images with reliance on L1 English sentences, and a preference to have only ASL used in classrooms. The function of learners thinking in English translation significantly correlated with reliance on L1 English words when learning new ASL signs, a preference for the use of both ASL and spoken English rather than only the use of English in classes, and a preferred emphasis on learning ASL grammar. The data suggests that language perceptual processing strategies significantly correlated with the learning strategies of different note-taking strategies, reliance on L1 English when learning ASL signs, preferred classroom language through which to learn ASL, and the linguistic area of study emphasized for learning ASL. Other learning strategies that pertain to learning activities and questioning sources did not significantly correlate with any of the language perceptual processing schemas.

The perceptual processing schemas did not involve the learning activities or the preferred answer sources for learner questions. There were, however, no significant correlations between the language processing schemas and other learning strategies. Apparently, those other learning strategies were related to the use of classroom resources and not to language processing.

Then, information regarding learners' preferred language perceptual processing schemas were correlated with their preferred learning strategies. Students with learning disabilities who preferred visual and auditory perceptual processing schemas tended to rely on textbooks and emphasized vocabulary learning. Learners with learning disabilities who preferred kinesthetic perceptual processing schemas tended to use spoken English to learn ASL and emphasize learning via discourse.

Chapter 4

Table 24. Correlations between Language Perceptual Processing Groups and Language Learning Strategies for Learners with Learning Disabilities.

	ThinkPicturesImages	ThinkEnglishTransl
Note-taking Strategies		
I draw pictures and images that describe new signs.	.298*	−.173
I put down actions that describe the new signs.	.027	−.062
I put down English words for new ASL signs.	−.100	.059
Reliance on L1 English		
Reliance on L1 English words	−.079	.420**
Reliance on L1 English sentences	.344*	−.188
Preferred Classroom Language		
To have both spoken English and ASL in classes	−.136	.277*
To have as much English as possible spoken in classes	−.088	−.343*
To have only ASL signed in classes	.288*	−.026
Preferred Learning Activities		
I give narrations.	.153	−.075
I do dialogues with other people in class.	.026	.199
I follow the student textbook.	.100	.053
I listen (watch) activities.	.033	.055
I do grammar exercises.	.097	.043
I play ASL games in class.	−.085	−.140
I do homework.	−.015	.096
I do project work.	.272	−.163
I translate from English to ASL.	.172	.171
I translate from ASL to English.	−.224	.069
Preferred Answer Sources for Learner Questions		
I ask the teacher.	a	a
I ask other students.	.165	.033
I look up textbook dictionary, Internet, CDs or videos.	.193	−.229
Preferred Linguistic Area of Study for Learning ASL		
I emphasize vocabulary.	−.015	−.025
I emphasize grammar.	−.027	.275*
I emphasize discourse.	.102	−.258

Notes:
*Correlation is significant at the 0.05 level (one-tailed).
**Correlation is significant at the 0.01 level (one-tailed).
[a] Level of significance cannot be calculated because there is no variance between groups.

LEARNING ASL AS A FOREIGN LANGUAGE

Comparisons of Language Processing Schemas and Language Strategies Used between General Education Learners and Learners with Learning Disabilities

The above information shows the motivation and language processing schema predictors of learning strategies for general education learners, and the language processing schema correlates of learning strategies for learners with learning disabilities. The relationship between language perceptual processing schemas and learning strategies are the only relationships compared to be able to ascertain any similar or different correlates of learning strategies between general education learners and learners with learning disabilities.

Visual processing of ASL entailed thinking in pictures when learning ASL signs. The general education learners who visually processed ASL preferred to take notes in pictures of new signs as memory aids. For learners with learning disabilities, this same visual processing of ASL significantly correlated with their taking notes in picture format, reliance on L1 English sentences when learning ASL grammar, and preference for having only ASL used as the main classroom communication mode.

General education learners who thought in actions emphasized learning grammar in ASL classes, preferred to note actions representing the new signs as memory aids, and preferred relying on the Internet, textbooks, and dictionaries for looking up signs. Learners with learning disabilities who preferred kinesthetic perceptual processing schemas tended to use spoken English for learning ASL and emphasized learning by use of discourse.

General education learners who thought of English translations for new signs and used auditory processes for learning ASL relied on L1 English words for processing ASL signs, and on L1 English sentences when processing new ASL sentences, and preferred that both ASL and English be used in ASL classrooms. Students with learning disabilities who used these auditory processing methods incorporated this processing mode into their learning in the same ways general education learners did.

Some learners used more than one sensory processing schema. General education learners who were both visual and auditory processers of ASL were predicted to prefer learning ASL by translating from ASL to English. Some learners with learning disabilities who processed ASL both visually and used aurally perceptual processing schemas tended to use textbooks and emphasize vocabulary learning.

Discussion

General Education Learners

To sum, the above results show that these learners had different motivation and language perceptual processing predictors for learning ASL than did learners with learning disabilities. Also, the study found these high school learners used three language perceptual processing schemas. A look at the regression analysis of predictors for learning strategies informs us that not all motivation and language perceptual processing variables served as predictors of learners' learning strategies. Different sets of predictors were found for the different language learning strategies. The study's findings are discussed in the following section in terms of the roles that motivation and/or language perceptual processing schemas had on learning.

Learners varied in how they used L1 English words and sentences when processing ASL signs and sentences. Some learners relied on using L1 English words if they thought of English translations when processing ASL signs. This suggests that these learners saw ASL grammar as a manual representation of English and, therefore, processed signs by seeking their equivalents in English. Other learners who saw ASL signs as a series of movements sought English motion word equivalents for ASL signs. Yet other learners relied on L1 English sentence structure if they thought of English translations when processing ASL sentences and held the perception that ASL was easy to learn. This suggests that these learners thought that ASL would be easier to learn because they held the perception that they only needed to seek sign equivalents for English and then use them in English grammatical order to communicate via ASL.

Learners differed in the language processing schemas they used when they preferred different communication modes in ASL classes. The learners who wanted both English and ASL used for classroom communication tended to think in English translations. These learners wanted to both understand ASL grammatical structure and thought of English words as

LEARNING ASL AS A FOREIGN LANGUAGE

ASL sign equivalents. Learners who wanted only voiced English used in ASL classes also thought in terms of English word equivalents for ASL signs. Some learners preferred using this same method because they had an intellectual interest in ASL structure and needed to use it for family communication. Other learners preferred classroom communication only in ASL. They seemed to want an understanding of ASL grammatical structure. Other learners preferring this classroom communication mode tended to think in terms of English translations for signs and needed to learn it for improving their English skills. Apparently, by watching teachers use ASL in classes, these learners translated ASL into English and presumably came to understand how concepts are lexicalized and grammaticalized into ASL sentence structure. They apparently wanted to apply this information into their learning of English structure.

Learners varied in the linguistic area of study in ASL they preferred for different possible reasons. Some learners preferred to learn ASL vocabulary if they perceived ASL as unique in its visual and manual modality. ASL vocabulary is made of lexical items. These learners apparently wanted to learn how to incorporate visual and manual representations of concepts into lexical signs. Learners preferring to learn ASL grammar tended to want to become ASL teachers, challenged themselves in learning ASL, and thought in actions when processing ASL. They apparently understood that ASL grammar differed from that of English and wanted to challenge themselves in learning a grammar using a modality different from English.

By thinking in actions when processing ASL, some learners may have seen ASL grammar as a sign system of movements and learned it by processing the gestural attributes of signs that approximate the movements of their referents. They also wanted to learn ASL grammar because of future plans to become ASL teachers.

Other learners wanted to learn ASL discourse rules if they had both an intellectual interest in the language and had performed poorly in other (spoken) foreign languages. That they wanted to use a foreign language in conversation, but did not do well in them, suggests that the method used in their learning of other foreign languages may have played a role in their poor classroom performance. These learners may have thought that they lacked sufficient opportunity for conversation in other foreign languages. That they also had an intellectual interest in ASL when they experienced poor classroom performance in other foreign languages suggests that they may have thought that ASL provided the linguistc means for conversations.

Students who took notes in picture format tended to think in pictures when processing ASL and found that learning ASL might help in career plans that involved working with D/HH people or in other deafness-related areas. They may also have wanted to carry this pictorial frame of reference into these careers. They may have felt that taking visual notes made learning ASL easier. Some learners made action notes also for similar reasons. The findings imply that both groups of learners felt that these methods helped them process concepts of ASL as a language. Still other learners preferred to take notes in English words if they thought of English translations when processing ASL signs. They apparently learned and processed ASL by translating ASL concepts into English.

Learners seemed to have had different reasons for preferring differing learning activities. There were no motivation or language perceptual processing predictors for doing narratives as a learning activity. Learners did narratives and told stories in ASL during class, regardless of their motivation for taking ASL or their preferred language perceptual schema for processing ASL. Students preferred to do dialogues if they saw ASL as unique. They wanted to learn how to use hands to visualize and communicate ideas with each other. Students preferring to learn ASL from textbooks tended to want to become ASL teachers. They viewed textbooks as providing ASL equivalents in English words and grammar. They seemed to want to incorporate this learning activity when teaching ASL. Learners who preferred to learn by watching teachers and classmates in class activities tended to want to work with D/HH people in the future. This suggests that the learners wanted to see how ASL was used by their teachers and classmates to help them learn how to communicate with D/HH people in future careers.

Learners preferred doing grammar exercises if they wanted to challenge themselves to learn ASL and thought in actions. They apparently wanted to take up learning the grammar of a language different from English. Learners preferring to play ASL games as a learning strategy tended to view ASL as unique and took it to learn about deaf people. For these learners, ASL games may have informed them of cultural activities within the signing D/HH community and given them an opportunity to converse in ASL. Learners preferring to do homework took ASL as a way of improving English language skills and as a way of helping them find English equivalents to ASL signs because these tended to be found in printed English. The learners who wanted to do projects saw ASL as unique, took it for purposes of future career plans, and for better communication with their families. Projects in ASL classrooms often consisted of learner research on topics pertaining to ASL and the American Deaf community and culture. These learners may have been fascinated with linguistic features of ASL and/or with the ASL-using D/HH community.

Learners varied in their preferred ways of obtaining answers to their questions. Learners preferred asking teachers for answers if they had an intellectual interest in ASL and viewed it as unique. They may have wanted information about the physical features of signs that correspond with visual concepts and how to produce ASL signs to represent these features. Learners preferred asking other learners if they viewed ASL as unique, needed it for communicating with family and friends, and had performed poorly in other foreign languages. This finding suggests that, while the learners felt a need to use ASL to communicate with their family and friends and see ASL as unique, they may have preferred to ask other learners and not their teachers for assistance since they had not done well in other languages. That they viewed ASL as unique suggests that they believed that ASL provided them with a visual and manual means to process concepts. Learners who preferred finding answers from dictionaries, the Internet, and textbooks thought of ASL as unique and as containing a system of actions. Information gained from these other sources tended to be written in English as well as in pictures and in video format. These learners apparently wanted to see how signers portrayed ASL on videos and used the mentioned sources to help them process ASL.

Learning ASL as a Second Language

ASL teachers employed these learning strategies in their classes. As seen, high school learners preferred different strategies for learning ASL. A learning strategy may relate to the language, community, and/or linguistic aspects of the language. Learners' learning strategy preferences were shown as related to their motivation for taking ASL and their language perceptual processing of different aspects of ASL. Motivation provided insights into the aspects of the language and community about which learners wanted to learn. Learners, therefore, preferred to learn areas that related to their reasons for taking ASL. Language perceptual processing of a language relates to how learners processed linguistic features of a language. As seen in the study, most learners processed information about language and community according to their preferred way of processing ASL. Motivation coupled with language perceptual processing generated learner language learning strategies. In some cases, either motivation or language perceptual processing, but not both, guided some learners' learning strategies. Also, learners varied in their motivations, language processing methods, and ASL learning strategies.

The study found that high school learners used the three language perceptual processing schemas of thinking of ASL in terms of pictures and images, actions, or via English translation. Barbe and Swassing (1979) and Dunn and Dunn (1979) stated that learners have three distinct perceptual processing forms, that is, visual, kinesthetic, and auditory, respectively, which dovetails with this study's findings. The findings are also in keeping with those of Peterson (2009), particularly in that ASL learners perceived ASL as a visual language and distinct from English. Peterson (2009), in his study of college-level ASL learners, found that learners agreed that spoken English and ASL be used as the language through which to learn ASL, that grammar instruction and vocabulary learning were important, and that they preferred asking their teachers if they had questions. This is reflected in this study's findings also.

This study shows that learners' motivations for learning ASL determined their learning strategy, as was true for the learners in the studies conducted by Oxford and Nyikos (1989), Mochizuki (1991), Nyikos and Oxford (1993), Chang and Huang (1999), Wharton (2000), and Chou (2002). Since the questionnaire items covered largely integrative motivation, results were compared with results in previous studies on integrative (also known as intrinsic) motivation. This study shows that integrative motivation was associated largely with cognitive and metacognitive learning strategies, which is supported by other study findings (Okada, Oxford, & Abo, 1996; Chen, 1999; Nakayama, 2005).

This study also found that learners' language perceptual processing of ASL shaped their learning strategies, which was also found in studies by Horowitz (1994), Garner and Alexander (1994), Garner and Hansis (1994) and Santiago (2009). Horwitz (1994) and Dörnyei (2005) who found that learners who visually processed a language preferred to receive information through sight and performed learning activities that required sight for information retrieval, such as reading words and seeing visual materials, support this study's findings. Other studies reached similar conclusions in other areas also. Learners who aurally processed a language preferred to receive information through hearing and performed learning activities that required speaking and hearing for information retrieval (Dörnyei, 2005; Oxford, 2003). Learners who kinesthetically processed a language preferred to receive information through bodily actions (Kinsella, 1995a; Kroonenberg, 1995; Dörnyei, 2005; Barbe & Swassing, 1979; Keefe, 1987). This study also found that some learners preferred multiple perceptual modality schemas when learning ASL.

Learners with Learning Disabilities

The results of the study are discussed in light of the relationship between preferred language perceptual processing schemas and preferred language learning strategies of learners with learning disabilities.

This study found learners with learning disabilities tended to use two language perceptual processing schemas for learning ASL—thinking in actions and thinking in a combination of pictures and English translation. This suggests that some learners with learning disabilities were visual processors of language, and others, auditory processors. These findings support Dunn and Dunn's (1979) assessment of learners' perceptual processing of language, in that learners perceived language in terms of its visual, auditory (words), as well as in kinesthetic (gestural) qualities. Previous studies demonstrated that learners identified as having learning disabilities and who took foreign language classes experienced difficulties learning the auditory-based phonology, orthography, speaking, and listening in both spoken native and foreign languages. This phenomenon was also found to be true of learners who were poor readers and did not have learning disabilities.

This study, however, found that learners with learning disabilities used visual and auditory processing schemas when learning ASL. This was not in keeping with study findings by Sparks and colleagues (Sparks, 1995; Sparks & Ganschow, 1993, 1995; Sparks, Ganschow, Javorsky, Pohlman, & Patton, 1992; Sparks, Ganschow, Kenneweg, & Miller, 1991; Sparks, Ganschow, & Pohlman, 1989; Sparks et al., 2006; Sparks et al., 2008). These studies found that learners' with learning disabilities in auditory processing of native languages have led to their experiencing problems in learning foreign languages also.

Language Learning Strategies

This study wanted to determine if learners' preferred language perceptual schema for processing a foreign language shaped the learning strategies they used. The above results show that learners with learning disabilities varied in their processing schemas and learning strategies. For instance, significant differences between learners using the two language perceptual processing schemas for learning ASL became apparent in their preference for spoken English for classroom communication, using textbooks, and their emphasis on learning vocabulary and discourse. This suggests that a relationship exists between learner learning disability, how learners processed ASL, and in learning strategies used.

Some of the above findings were similar to those of previous studies. For instance, the fact most of this study's learners preferred to learn ASL vocabulary and discourse was also found to be the case in Peterson's (2009) studies. Previous studies also attested to the difficulties learners with learning disabilities and learners without learning disabilities who were poor readers had with processing both foreign and native languages via auditory means. These studies also found that this, in turn, affected their processing of spoken and graphemic information from speaking, listening, and reading foreign languages (Dinklage, 1971; Sparks, 1995; Sparks & Ganschow, 1993, 1995; Sparks, Ganschow, Javorsky, Pohlman, & Patton, 1992; Sparks, Ganschow, Kenneweg, & Miller, 1991; Sparks,

Ganschow, & Pohlman, 1989; DeFino & Lombardino, 2004; Barrera, 2003; Ganschow et al., 1998; Sparks et al., 2006; Sparks et al., 2008).

This study also showed that the learners with learning disabilities taking ASL classes generated different schemas for processing languages. The presumption of other studies such as conducted by Sparks and colleagues (Sparks, 1995; Sparks & Ganschow, 1993, 1995; Sparks, Ganschow, Javorsky, Pohlman, & Patton, 1992; Sparks, Ganschow, Kenneweg, & Miller, 1991; Sparks, Ganschow, & Pohlman, 1989; Sparks et al., 2006; Sparks et al., 2008) that all learners with learning disabilities process foreign languages in the same way did not hold in this study. Learners reported that their varying perceptual processing of foreign languages shaped their strategies for learning foreign languages.

Comparisons of Language Processing Correlates of Learning Strategies between General Education Learners and Learners with Learning Disabilities

Similarities and differences were found regarding language processing correlates of learning strategies between general education learners and learners with learning disabilities. Both groups thought in pictures when learning ASL signs and preferred to take notes in pictures of new signs as memory aids. However, learners with learning disabilities needed to simultaneously rely on L1 English sentences when learning ASL grammar. Both groups of learners thought in actions when learning signs. However, general education learners who thought in actions looked for signs in print materials and the Internet, and emphasized learning grammar and doing grammar exercises. By contrast, learners with learning disabilities needed the use of spoken English and emphasized learning discourse. Both groups also thought of English translation when learning new signs and did so in similar ways. They mostly thought of L1 English words and felt that both ASL and English should be used as classroom communication languages. General education learners relied on L1 English sentences to think of English translations for new signs. Learners with learning disabilities reported that they thought of English translations when learning new grammar. Some general education learners and learners with learning disabilities used more than one sensory processing schema. However, they differed as to which ones they used. General education learners used visual and auditory processing schemas for learning ASL by translation of signs into English. Learners with learning disabilities used multisensory schemas to learn ASL vocabulary and tended to learn from textbooks.

Results of this study suggested that learners with learning disabilities used several perceptual language processing schemas for learning ASL. These learners also varied in which learning strategies they used. Different explanations based on perceptual language processing schemas were given as to why learners with learning disabilities preferred certain learning strategies. Peterson (2009) found, in his study of college-level ASL learners, that learners agreed that spoken English and ASL be used as ASL classroom communication languages, that grammar instruction and vocabulary learning were important, and that they tended to ask their teachers if they had questions, which agrees with this study's findings. Learners in this study reported that ASL teachers should focus mainly on teaching ASL grammar while learners in Peterson's study felt it was important, but should not be emphasized in classroom instruction. No perception predictors existed for other learning strategies listed on the questionnaire.

Pedagogical Implications for Learners With and Without Learning Disabilities

Results of this study suggest that teachers use differentiated instruction methods for ASL learners to match learner motivation, language perceptual processing schema, and learning strategies. All learners in this study could hear and speak. It cannot be assumed that they were equally motivated to learn ASL and were auditory processors of linguistic information. Students reported different reasons for taking ASL and varied in their perceptual processing of the language. This has implications for learning strategies they used in ASL classes. Teachers need to know which learning strategies learners use for learning ASL. This information will assist them in using instruction methods that match learners' preferred learning strategies.

Teachers also need to know why learners use certain learning strategies over others in relation to learners' motivations and perceptions so they can determine which linguistic areas and which aspects of the language community will appeal most to learners. In essence, teachers need to match instruction to learners' interests and perceptual processing strengths (Dunn 1983).

L2 learners' preferred method of processing of ASL influences the type of instructional methods used in ASL classes and the grades that learners receive. Teachers may need to use instructional strategies that enable learners who prefer learning ASL visually to match signs and related concepts with visual representations, such as pictures and videos. For learners who prefer learning ASL via auditory means, teachers may need to incorporate auditory means, such as spoken and written English, so that learners can learn how to match signs with related concepts. For these learners, ASL teachers may need to gradually help them transition from dependence on the auditory dimension to relying more on visual means for processing and learning ASL. It is hoped that this study's results in learners' preference for certain learning strategies as determined by their motivation and preferred language perceptual processing schema will aid ASL teachers in pedagogical planning.

This study's results also have implications for the kind of course materials that teachers use and their incorporation of various learning activities. The correlations discerned in this study were grounded on the basis that ASL teachers used a content- and task-based communication approach. This approach, described previously, affects how teachers teach topics pertaining to daily life, the Deaf community and culture, how they introduce ASL signs and grammar, and how they construct conversational tasks so that learners could improve their skills in using ASL signs and grammar. Teachers incorporated the learning activities discussed previously. Teachers gave grades to learners based on their performance in receptive, expressive, and dialogue examinations, homework, projects, presentations, and class attendance.

Finally, the results of this study suggest that differentiated instruction strategies may help learners with learning disabilities if teachers consider their differing perceptions and learning processes in class planning and instruction. For instance results of the study demonstrate that learners with learning disabilities use perceptual schemas other than via auditory means. These findings may also assist high school and college disability advisors in their foreign language recommendations to learners with learning disabilities, particularly in regard to ASL.

5

LEARNER ACHIEVEMENT

Learner achievement is the ultimate goal of foreign language education. Past studies were conducted that explored and assessed criteria for attaining high learner achievement. They have focused on, among other criteria, learners' motivation, language processing, and learning strategies as possible determinants of learners' foreign language course performance. The issue is whether learners' motivation, language processing schemas, and learning strategies were associated with their course grade achievement.

This study explores the relationship between L2 American Sign Language (ASL) learners' motivation, language perceptual processing schema, and preferred learning strategy with their course grade achievement. No study existed until this one regarding ASL that explored these relationships with respect to the language, however. The following section reviews previous studies that explored these relationships and learner course achievement in spoken L2 languages. These study findings may have implications for studying the above-indicated areas in relationship to ASL course achievement.

Previous studies varied in measures of achievement used. Some focused on proficiency levels as measured by tests in language proficiency. Others focused on language comprehension levels as measured by assessment procedures, such as grammar tests, receptive tests, expressive tests, and stimuli-response tests. Still others provided course grades as a measure of a combination of proficiency levels, receptive and expressive quizzes, homework, projects, and attendance records. This study utilized learners' course grades as an indicator of achievement.

Variables in the Relationship between Learners' Motivation and Achievement

Prior L2 research literature explored variables that shape learners' course grade achievement. Some researchers saw motivation as a variable contributing to learners' learning and achievement in foreign language classes. A number of studies employed Gardner's *AMTB* to find out which motivation variables applied to several groups of L2 learners and assessed the relationship between motivation and achievement. Lalonde and Gardner (1985), using the *AMTB* and measures of French achievement, found that integrative motivation was the predictor of French class grades and achievement test scores. Ushioda (2004) studied learners' attitudes and motivation in second language learning in online language courses and used a modified *AMTB*. She found that learners' motivation was significantly connected to achievement test scores. Gardner, Lalonde, and Moorcroft (1985) found that indices of integrative motivation correlated with indices of L2 achievement. Later studies found that subjects who scored high in language aptitude, had integrative motivation, and a good learning rate were able to learn language more quickly than those who did not. For instance, the Gardner, Masgoret, Tennant, and Mihic (2004), Csizer and Dörnyei (2005), and Oller, Hudson, and Liu (1977) studies all showed that higher levels of positive attitude and integrative motivation generated higher achievement. Masgoret and Gardner (2003) performed a meta-analysis of studies conducted by Gardner and associates and saw that correlations between motivation and achievement were uniformly high.

Other studies discovered that instrumental motivation generated higher learner achievement. Lukmani (1972) studied native Marathi-speaking high school learners learning English, and looked at their English proficiency and the nature of their motivation for learning the language. Sixty girls from a graduating high school class participated in the study. The learners were a part of a community in the non-Westernized section of Mumbai, India, and Marathi was the community's language and the language of instruction at the high school. Results of the study questionnaires showed that learners instrumentally motivated to learn English performed significantly higher on English proficiency evaluations than the learners who were integratively motivated. Lukmani (1972) explained that the Marathi speakers took English because they sought modern ideas and information about lifestyles represented in the English-speaking world as ways of improving their communities.

Some studies show variations across L1 groups in their motivation and achievement of foreign languages. Tachibana, Matsukawa, and Zhong (1996) studied Japanese and Chinese high school learners and discovered that Japanese learners were integratively motivated to learn English as a language, about its culture and people, and achieved higher scores than Chinese high school learners who were more pragmatically oriented toward studying English as a crucial aspect for their futures.

Still other studies did not find that motivation is related to higher learner achievement. Teitelbaum et. al. (1975) studied learners' ethnic attitudes and their acquisition of Spanish as a second language. A Cloze test of Spanish proficiency and a questionnaire about linguistics and ethnic attitudes were administered to 116 learners in their third semester of Spanish at the University of New Mexico. Teitelbaum et al. (1975) found that an integrative motivation index and positive orientation toward the local Chicano community were not prerequisites for successful Spanish language acquisition. Gardner, Masgoret, Tennant, and Mihic (2004) added that learners' learning experiences shaped their performance more than did their motivation. Clement and Kruidenier (1985), in a study of francophone Canadian high school learners, found that aptitude, to a greater degree than motivation, determined linguistic outcomes. Vandergrift (2005) studied the relationships among motivation, metacognition, and proficiency in listening comprehension among adolescent French learners and found that listening proficiency correlated negatively with learners' motivation and that correlations with intrinsic and extrinsic motivation were not as high as anticipated. Ushioda (2007) examined the relationship between integrative and instrumental motivation measures and achievement scores on a Japanese language test among Southern California community college learners. Results showed no statistically significant relationship between integrative motivation scores and Japanese language test scores. Also, no statistically significant relationship was detected between instrumental motivation scores and Japanese language test scores.

One study in the relationship between motivation and achievement in ASL was conducted. Lang, Foster, Gustina, Mowl, and Lui (1996a,b) claimed, in their study, that they found high achievers in ASL held positive cultural attitudes and had integrative motivation. Those learners who did not attain high levels of ASL proficiency held negative, more medically-oriented attitudes toward deaf people, They demonstrated instrumental motivational orientations. However, the study did not provide data and statistics showing the relationship between motivation and achievement in ASL learners.

The above studies show mixed results on the relationship between motivation and achievement. Some studies showed that different types of motivation shape varying degrees of learner achievement. Other studies did not. It is possible that other variables, such as learners' language processing and learning strategies, affect the motivation-achievement relationship. This study examines the relationship between motivation and learner performance in ASL classes.

Language Processing Schema and Achievement

Learners' perceptual processing of language is another learner variable that shapes learning in foreign language classes. One study investigated the relationship between preferred perceptual learning style, language learning strategy used, and English achievement. Hou (2009) studied college EFL learners and used measures, such as the *Strategy Inventory for Language Learning* (SILL, Oxford, 1990), the *Perceptual Learning Style Preference Questionnaire* (PLSP, Reid, 1984), and the *National English Test in Proficiency for all on the Web* (NETPAW, Chuang, 2004). Hou found that learners showed variation in their preferred language perceptual processing schemas, and that learners who favored auditory processing schema and auditory-based learning strategies achieved higher English language achievement.

The question now was whether ASL learners' perceptual processing of ASL had any effect on their course achievement and acquisition of ASL. Since no study prior to this one had investigated the relationship between language perceptual processing schemas and learners' course grade achievement in ASL as a foreign language, this study seeks to obtain data about this relationship.

CHAPTER 5

Learning Strategy and Achievement

L2 studies discovered a wide range of correlations between language learning strategy and learner performance. Dreyer and Oxford (1996) and Park (1997) employed Oxford's SILL and TOEFL tests and found that the higher the *SILL* scores, the higher the *TOEFL* test scores. Gardner, Tremblay, and Masgoret (1997) replicated the above findings. Other studies looked at the relationship between certain learning strategies and course achievement. Chen (2008) and Chiang (2005) found that vocabulary learning strategies improved learners' reading in a foreign language. Moreover, learners used rehearsal strategies most frequently, while encoding strategies were less frequently used. Chiang (2005) added that vocabulary size had an effect on the use of vocabulary learning strategies. Statistically significant differences were found between vocabulary size and a belief that words should be memorized, as well as the learning strategies of self-initiation, visual activation, and repetition of word structure and association. Minggui and Yu (2005) revealed significant relationships between cognitive and self-regulated strategies and English academic achievement, and no significant relationships among communicative and social strategies and English academic achievement. Sungwoo (2000) found only weak relationships between language learning strategies and language proficiency. The metacognitive and cognitive learning strategies and language proficiency factors varied across different proficiency level groups. Social and affective strategies were found not to determine high achievement.

Other studies discovered no relationship between learning strategies and learner achievement. Politzer and McGroarty (1985) and Oxford and Ehrman (1995) found low correlations between *SILL* and proficiency ratings, and Mullins (1992) found no relationship between *SILL* and GPA and language placement test scores. Nisbet et al. (2005) added that only metacognitive strategy correlated with *TOEFL*. Kang (2000) employed *TOEFL* and a questionnaire about language learning strategies. He found weak relationships between language learning strategies and language proficiency. Only 13% and 15% of the variance of the listening and grammar/reading factor were explained by the language teaming strategies. Nisbet (2003) also employed *SILL* and *TOEFL* and discovered that a combination of two learning strategies, metacognitive strategies and affective strategies, accounted for only 4% of the variation in *ITP-TOEFL* score. Soric and Ancic (2008) added that relationships between learning strategies and causal attributions were very complex, and that the patterns of these relationships between learning strategy and achievement were quite different for different learners and also for successful and unsuccessful learners.

Results in the above studies show moderate to strong correlations between learner performance and the use of linguistic strategies, cognitive strategies, and metacognitive strategies, but weak correlations between learner performance and affective and social strategies. As these studies are limited to spoken second languages, what remains was to determine the correlates between learning strategies and L2 ASL learner performance. This study sought correlates between learner responses to questions about learning strategies and teachers' reports on learner performance. Correlations of these reports with learning strategies were tested for significance of the relationship.

Previous Studies of Motivation, Language Processing Schema, and Learning Strategy Relationships with Learner Achievement Levels

Studies that discussed learner course achievement sought its correlates and predictors for instructional designs and other pedagogical purposes. Studies also explored extra-educational correlates and predictors of achievement. Past studies identified personal health issues and socio-economic status, especially poverty, as extra-educational correlates and predictors (e.g., Perera, 2006; Sung, 2009). The interest here was on the intra-educational correlates and predictors. These show the dimensions of learner interest and learning as predictors of achievement.

A few studies explored the interplay among achievement and learners' motivation, language perceptual processing schema, and learning strategies. Macaro (2001) found that LLS were linked to proficiency levels, and that other factors, such as learners' linguistic resources and motivation contributed to their achievement. Chou (2002), in an exploratory study of EFL Taiwanese technological and vocational college learners' language learning strategies and the relationship of these strategies to motivation and language proficiency, used *SILL* and questionnaires concerning learners' demographics and motivation. He found that learners' strategy use was strongly correlated with motivation and language proficiency. Learners with higher proficiency in English used more learning strategies than those who achieved lower proficiency levels. Flemens (2009), using *SILL* and *AMTB*, also discovered that language-learning strategy use and motivation correlated highly with language proficiency. In addition, attitudes toward learning a foreign language, years spent studying it, motivational intensity (a measure of integrative motivation), grade level, and affective strategies served as explanatory variables of expected course grades, with motivational intensity as the most important predictor. The analysis of individual language-learning strategies indicated metacognitive and affective strategies as also being significant predictors of expected course grades. The other strategies were found as insignificant predictors of expected course grades.

Macaro (2001), Chou (2002), and Flemens (2009) also found that the number of learning strategies learners used shaped their course performance, and that language-related learning strategies ensured higher learner performance. These studies were conducted with college-level learners of spoken foreign languages. Results of this study will be compared with the findings of the above-mentioned studies.

Achievement of Learners with Learning Disabilities

As mentioned previously, the aim of foreign language learning for learners with learning disabilities is to have them acquire and master a language for communication purposes as is the case with learners without learning disabilities. L2 studies found a wide range of correlations between learning strategy and learner performance. The problem with these L2 studies is that they covered learners with different learning disabilities, without identifying which types of learning disabilities generated the type of foreign language learning difficulties they experienced. Learners with learning disabilities varied in the types of difficulty they experienced in learning foreign languages. Also, learning disabilities were not identified for learners who achieved foreign language learning successes. Individual differences are at play in second language learning. There are different types of language processing problems. Previous studies of all learning difficulties experienced by learners with learning disabilities focused on spoken foreign languages, not ASL. No study had previously been done on the relationship between language processing schemas, learning strategies used, and performance by learners with learning disabilities in ASL as a foreign language.

Learning ASL as L2 for learners whose first languages are spoken presents issues of modality differences between spoken and signed languages. For this study, the issues are whether learning ASL requires perceptual processing schemas that are different from those used in the processing of spoken foreign languages; and whether learners with learning disabilities needed to use different perceptual processing methods for learning ASL than they may have used in learning spoken foreign languages. Also, the impact of language processing and learning strategies used by these learners had on learner performance was studied.

Study Methods Regarding Learner Achievement in Learning ASL

Statistics were employed to ascertain the strength of relationships between the dependent variable of learners' course grades and the independent variables of learner motivation, language perceptual processing schema, and learning strategies.

Study Results of Learner Achievement in Learning ASL

General Education Learners

Teachers submitted learner course grades for analysis. A number of learners did not receive grades because they did not complete ASL courses during the study period. It is for this reason that 22 questionnaires out of 217 were eliminated 195 questionnaires remained for further analysis of the relationship between these predictors and learners' course grades. Ages of the learners who completed the questionnaire, and whose grades were submitted to the researcher, ranged from 13 to 18 years old, with a mean of 15.2 years old. Sixty-one percent of learners were female and 39% were male. Forty-five percent of the learner-respondents were in ASL Level 1 classes, 33% in Level 2, and close to 22% in Level 3 classes. Sixty-four percent of these learners were Caucasian and approximately 34% were

Chapter 5

of different ethnicities, with 3 missing cells for answers related to ethnicity in learners' questionnaire responses. Most learners, 79.5%, spoke only one language, and 18.6% of the learners spoke more than one language, with 4 missing cells in learners' questionnaire answers. English was the first spoken language of 90.5% of learner respondents and 7.1% of learners spoke other languages, with 5 missing cells in learner answers about this.

To assess learners' grade scores at the end of terms across schools, descriptive statistics with grade mean and standard deviation were performed. Table 25 below shows mean grade scores and standard deviations, and significance levels, of learners of different age, gender, and ASL level groups across schools.

The study revealed differences between some learners' grades within age, gender, and ASL course level subgroups across the schools. To assess whether these differences were significant in grade score mean for these subgroups, ANOVA tests were employed and results showed significant differences in learners' grade mean for age ($F(5,189) = 5.674$, $p < .001$),

Table 25. Mean Course Grades and Standard Deviations for Age, Gender, and ASL Course Level Groups Across Schools for General Education Learners.

	N	Mean	SD
Total	195	84.16	8.16
Age			
13 years old	7	65.43	17.29
14 years old	58	80.55	16.79
15 years old	55	82.60	13.33
16 years old	44	85.55	13.18
17 years old	29	91.41	7.67
18 years old	2	65.00	7.07
Gender			
Males	73	73.66	16.36
Females	122	88.86	10.08
ASL Level			
Level 1	87	80.61	17.36
Level 2	65	83.05	13.24
Level 3	43	88.54	8.69

Note: SD refers to standard deviation
N = number of students.

gender (F(1,193) = 64.533, p < .001), and ASL course level (F(2,192) = 4.308, p < .05) subgroups. In addition, LSD post-hoc tests were used to assess the significance of the differences in grade means for these same subgoups. Significant differences occurred between 13-year-olds and 15-year-olds, 16-year-olds and 17-year-olds, each at $p = .000$. The lowest achievement scores were attained by the 13- and 18-year-olds, and the highest scores were attained by 17-year-olds, followed by 16-, 15- and 14-year-olds. Female learners had significantly higher grade means than did male learners. In addition, a significant difference in grade means ($p = .000$) was discerned between learners in ASL level 3 classes, who received higher grades than did learners in ASL level 1 courses; these learners received the lowest grades. No significant differences in grade means between learners in other age and ASL course level subgroups were found.

ANOVA statistics were employed to ascertain whether there was an interaction between schools, and the age, gender, and ASL course levels of learners, For age as independent variable, learner grades as dependent variable, and school as covariate, the statistic was F (4) = 0.793, p = .531. For gender as an independent variable, learner grades as a dependent variable, and school as covariate, the statistic was F (2) = 2.371, p = .097. For ASL course level as an independent variable, learner grades as a dependent variable, and school as covariate, the statistic was F (3) = 0.612, p = .608. These F statistics show that there was no significant difference between schools in the learners' mean grades for age, gender, and ASL course levels. These results suggest that there were no interaction effects between schools and age, gender, and ASL course levels on learners' grade performances. Learners' grades and responses to questionnaire items could then be used to analyze further the relationship between grades and motivation, language processing, and learning strategies of all learners in the study schools.

The next step was to find which motivation factors, language perceptual processing schemas, and learning strategies contributed to higher learner grade performance for all schools. Two-tailed Spearman correlation statistic was used to assess these areas. Table 26 shows results on correlations between learner grade achievement and their motivation, language perceptual processing schema and learning strategies used by general education learners for all schools.

CHAPTER 5

Table 26. Correlations between General Education Learners' Preferred Motivation, Language Perceptual Processing Schemas, Learning Strategies, and Course Achievement.

Correlation Factors	Correlation with Learners' Grades
Motivation	
Intellectual interest in the language	−.347**
ASL is a unique language that I want to learn	−.284**
I want to challenge myself in learning the language	−.273**
Career plans	−.154*
I want to learn about deaf people	−.226**
I want to work with deaf people in the future	−.239**
I want to become a teacher of ASL in the future	−.162*
It is easier to learn a foreign language	−.198**
ASL helps me learn and use English better	.065
ASL is easier to learn than other foreign languages	.023
I did not do well in other foreign languages	.219**
My guidance counselor asks me to take ASL	.085
I need to communicate with family and friends	−.019
I want to communicate with my family	.019
I want to communicate with my friends	−.059
Language Perceptual Processing Schemas	
I think of pictures and images that describe the new signs.	−.066
I think of actions that describes the new signs.	−.097
I think of its English translation.	−.008
Learning Strategies	
Reliance on L1 Language	
I think of English words when I learn new ASL signs.	.031
I think of English sentences when I learn new ASL sentences.	.065
Note-taking Strategies	
I draw pictures and images that describe new signs.	.032
I put down actions that describe the new signs.	−.156*
I put down English words for new ASL signs.	.056
Classroom Language for Learning ASL	
To have a combination of ASL and English spoken.	.129
To have as much English as possible spoken.	.348**
To have only ASL signed.	−.107

Achievement in Learning ASL as a Foreign Language

Learning Activities

I give narrations.	−.055
I do dialogues with other people in class.	−.015
I follow the learners' textbook.	.031
I listen (watch) activities.	−.076
I do grammar exercises.	−.114
I play ASL games in class.	−.235**
I do homework.	.063
I do project work.	−.143*
I translate from English to ASL.	.126
I translate from ASL to English.	−.028

Sources for Answers to Learner Questions

I ask the teacher.	−.246**
I ask other students.	−.018
I look up in the textbook dictionary, internet, CDs, or videos.	−.021

Linguistic Area of Study for Learning ASL

I emphasize vocabulary.	−.215**
I emphasize grammar.	−.200**
I emphasize discourse.	−.071

Note: Figures are in Spearman Correlation Coefficients.
*$p < .05$ **$p < .01$ ***$p < .001$

Correlations Between General Education Learners' Preferred Motivations and Course Grades

The statistics behind the below information about correlations can be found in table 26. Correlations were based on ascending learners' grades and descending levels of importance in relation to questionnaire items. The items inversely correlated with learner grades were associated with higher learner grades. There were inverse and moderately strong correlations between learner grades and some motivation variables. These variables include intellectual interest in the language, ASL as a unique language, and challenge to self in learning ASL. Other motivation variables had inverse correlations as well. They were learning about deaf people, wanting to work with deaf people, wanting to become ASL teachers, and the perception that ASL is easier to learn than a spoken foreign language. These inverse correlations were significant because the motivation

CHAPTER 5

variables most important to learners, per their questionnaire responses, were associated with higher learner grades.

Some inversely weak correlations between learner grades and motivation variables were also found. These variables included the need to communicate with family and friends and wanting to communicate with friends. While these motivation variables were associated with higher learner grade scores, none of these inverse and weak correlations were significant.

There were positive correlations, albeit weak, between grades and some motivation variables. These included that ASL helped learners learn and use English better, the perception that ASL was easier to learn than other foreign languages, not doing well in other foreign languages, guidance counselor suggestions that some learners take ASL, and learners' wanting to communicate with family. These variables that learners considered as most important were associated with lower learner grades. However, these correlations were weak and not significant. They did not connect with higher learner grades. The only positive correlation between learner grades and the motivation variables was learners' not doing well in other foreign languages. This correlation was significant and associated with lower learner grades.

Correlations Between Learners' Preferred Language Perceptual Schemas and Course Grades

Some language perceptual processing schema correlations were insignificant and only weakly correlated with higher learner grades. These schemas included thinking in pictures, thinking of actions, and thinking of English translations of signs.

Correlations Between Learners' Preferred Learning Strategies and Course Grades

Learning strategies included the seven areas identified in the research literature. They were note-taking, reliance on L1 languages, preferred language for learning ASL, learning activities, questioning sources, and preferred linguistic level of ASL to learn.

There were positive, but weak and insignificant, correlations between learner grades and reliance on the L1 language learning strategies of thinking of English words when learning new signs and thinking of

English sentences when learning new ASL sentences. Other learning strategies also were positive, but weak, and not significantly correlated with higher learner grades. They were learners' note-taking strategies of drawing pictures and putting down English words for new ASL signs. However, the note-taking strategy variable of putting down actions for describing new signs was positively, significantly, but weakly correlated and was associated with higher learner grades.

Correlations between learner grades and preferred language for learning ASL were mixed. Positive, but weak and insignificant, correlations with learner grades were found for the preference for having a combination of ASL and English spoken in class. This strategy was not significantly associated with lower learner grades. The variable of preferring to have as much English as possible spoken in class was positively, significantly, and moderately correlated and was associated with lower learner grades. Also, the variable of preferring to have only ASL used in class was inversely, but weakly, correlated, and did not significantly correlate with higher learner grades.

Correlations Between Learners' Preferred Learning Activities and Course Grades

Results show that higher and lower learner performance correlated with learners' preferred learning activities. An inverse correlation was found between learner grades and learners' preferred learning activities of giving narrations, doing dialogues with classmates, listening and watching activities, doing grammar exercises, and translating from ASL to English. However, these correlations were weak, insignificant, and not associated with higher learner grades. Positive, and weak and insignificant, correlations were also found for the learning activities of using learner textbooks doing homework, and translating from English to ASL and learner grades. These correlations were not associated with lower learner grades. By contrast, correlations between learner grades and the learning activities of playing ASL games and doing project work were inverse, somewhat moderate, and significant. These correlations were associated with higher learner grades.

Inverse correlations were discerned between learner grades and strategies learners used in obtaining answers to course questions.

Some preferred asking teachers; others preferred to ask other learners; and yet others preferred looking answers up in textbooks, dictionaries, on the Internet, CDs, or videos. Only the learning strategy of asking questions of teachers had a somewhat moderately strong, but significant correlation, with higher learner grades. The other two correlations were weak, insignificant, and not associated with higher learner grades.

The preferred ASL linguistic areas of study of learner emphasis on learning vocabulary, learner emphasis on learning grammar, and learner emphasis on learning ASL via discourse were inversely correlated with learner grades. The preferred variables of emphasizing vocabulary and emphasizing grammar were moderately strong, significantly correlated, and associated with higher learner grades. The variable of emphasizing learning via discourse was weakly correlated and not associated with higher learner grades.

Learners with Learning Disabilities

The next area to be determined was whether learners' with learning disabilities preferred language perceptual processing schemas and language learning strategies were connected to their course achievement. As with the general education learners, correlations were conducted to assess the relationship between learners' grades and their preferred language processing schemas and preferred learning strategies. One-tailed Pearson correlation was used for assessing these relationships. Table 27 shows the results.

Correlations Between Learners' Preferred Learning Strategies and Course Grades

Grades were positively and significantly correlated with the learning strategies of putting down actions that describe new signs, playing ASL games in class, and asking questions of teachers. Negative, yet significant, correlations were found between the strategy of translating from ASL to English and learner grades. Learners' language perceptual schemas for processing ASL signs and other possible learning strategies did not contribute to higher or lower course achievement.

Table 27. Correlations between Course Grades, Preferred Thinking Strategies, and Language Learning Strategies for Learners with Learning Disabilities.

	Course Grades
Thinking Strategies	
I think in pictures and images.	.107
I think in actions.	.054
I think in English translation.	.010
Note-taking Strategies	
I draw pictures and images that describe new signs.	.068
I put down actions that describe the new signs.	.354*
I put down English words for new ASL signs.	−.115
Reliance on L1 English	
Reliance on L1 English words	.200
Reliance on L1 English sentences	.041
Classroom Language for Learning ASL	
To have both spoken English and ASL in classes	−.243
To have as much English as possible spoken in classes	.020
To have only ASL signed in classes	−.048
Learner Learning Activities	
I give narrations.	−.204
I do dialogues with other people in class.	−.050
I follow the learners' textbook.	.125
I listen (watch) activities.	.153
I do grammar exercises.	−.162
I play ASL games in class.	a***
I do homework.	.036
I do project work.	−.043
I translate from English to ASL.	.209
I translate from ASL to English.	−.292*
Sources for Answers to Learner Questions	
I ask the teacher.	a***
I ask other learners.	.187
I look up textbook dictionary, internet, CDs or videos.	−.104
Preferred Linguistic Area of Study for Learning ASL	
I emphasize vocabulary.	.186
I emphasize grammar.	.217
I emphasize discourse.	−.181

Notes:
*Correlation is significant at the 0.05 level (one-tailed).
**Correlation is significant at the 0.01 level (one-tailed).
[a]Level of significance cannot be calculated because there is no variance between groups.

Chapter 5

Discussion

General Education Learners

Study results are discussed in light of the relationship between preferred learner motivations, preferred language perceptual processing schemas, and preferred language learning strategies in relation to course achievement. Results showed that schools participating in the study did not differ significantly from each other in learners' mean grade scores. However, significant differences in learners' grade scores within age, gender, and ASL course levels were found across the schools. Thirteen- and 18-year-old learners had the lowest grades and 17-year-old learners had the highest grades. Female learners achieved higher grades than did male learners. Learners in higher ASL level courses scored higher than did learners in lower level courses. In addition, there is no interaction between schools and age, gender, and ASL course levels. These results are not surprising, considering that older learners, females, and learners in higher ASL level courses were interested in careers working with D/HH people, which by itself generated higher grades. Also, teacher pedagogies between participating schools were similar, which, not surprisingly, mitigated pedagogical influences on learners' grades.

Findings in this study were mixed in terms of agreement with those of other related studies. This study found that integrative motivations were highly correlated with high learner course grade achievement. This finding was similar to the study findings of Lalonde and Gardner (1985), Ushioda (2004), Gardner, Lalonde, and Moorcroft (1985), Gardner, Masgoret, Tennant, and Mihic (2004), Csizer and Dörnyei (2005), Tachibana, Matsukawa, and Zhong (1996), Oller, Hudson, and Liu (1977), Wen (1997), and Masgoret and Gardner (2003). Integrative motivation was also found to be highly correlated with learner course grade achievement, particularly in relation to learners' career aspirations of working with D/HH people. This finding concurred with findings in studies by Lukmani (1972). This study found, as did a study done by Lang, Foster, Gustina, Mowl, and Lui (1996a,b), that integrative motivation was associated with high levels of ASL proficiency.

This study found weak, but insignificant, correlations between learners' language perceptual processing schema and their level of course achievement. This contrasts with Hou's (2009) study that found learners' use of auditory perceptual strategies generated higher achievement in ESL. This study's findings dovetailed with those of Chou (2002) and Soric and Ancic (2008) in that learning strategies used correlate with learners' foreign language performance. Data from this study show several correlations between learning strategy and student learners' course grade achievement that agreed with findings in previous studies. This study found that learners using more learning strategies than others achieved higher course grades. This is in keeping with studies done by Takeuchi (1993), Dreyer and Oxford (1996), and Park (1997). However, studies by Politzer and McGroarty (1985), Oxford and Ehrman (1995), and Mullins (1992) did not agree with these findings. This study agreed with those of Chen (2008) and Chiang (2005) in that the use of vocabulary learning strategies are associated with higher course achievement. Nisbet's study (2003) found that metacognitive and affective learning strategies correlated with high learner achievement, which is in agreement with this study's findings. The Sungwoo (2000) and Kang (2000) studies found that no, or weak, relationships existed between language learning strategies and language proficiency, which differs from this study's findings in that area. These two studies also found that the metacognitive, cognitive, and language proficiency factors did not vary across different learner proficiency levels, which were also not like the findings of this study. Minggui and Yu (2005) found there were no significant correlations between communicative and social strategies, also not in keeping with this study's findings. This study also found that a combination of positive motivation and metacognitive and affective learning strategies contributes to learners' course achievement, which agreed with the findings of Macaro (2001) and Flemens (2009). That there are agreements and disagreements in results between the studies, including this one, suggests that the relationship between learning strategy and course achievement may be complicated by possible causes such as differences in learner demographics, education level, measure of student proficiency, and components of language learning strategies among the studies.

Learners with Learning Disabilities

Some of the study's findings agreed with findings in other studies, and some findings did not. Sparks and colleagues (Sparks & Ganschow, 1991; Sparks et al., 1993; Sparks, Ganschow, & Patton, 2008; Ganschow et al., 1998; Ganschow et al., 2000) found that the difficulties experienced by learners with learning disabilities were not due to aptitude, motivation, anxiety, attitude, or cognitive abilities, but, instead, were due to their processing of languages. That is, if learners with learning disabilities have difficulties in processing their native languages, this will carry over to their processing of foreign languages, particularly spoken ones (Sparks, in press; Mabbott, 1994). These other studies posited that transfer of language processing difficulties from native to second languages does occur. Sparks, Ganschow and Pohlman (1989) and Sparks and Ganschow (1991) proposed a Linguistic Coding Deficient Hypothesis (LCDH) as an explanatory model for the transfer of learning disabilities from native language to foreign languages, and that native language deficiencies generate foreign language deficiencies. Sparks' LCDH, however, is based on spoken language processing, not that of manual languages.

This study found that preferred perceptual schema for processing ASL and learning strategies for processing ASL did not affect learners with learning disabilities' attaining of higher ASL course grades. This study demonstrates that these learners' learning difficulties did not affect their ASL course performance and were not due to their learning disabilities. There was no instance of learners with learning disabilities exhibiting problems with linguistic coding in ASL. This may be explained by the fact that ASL teachers used multi-modality approaches in class.

ASL teachers employed a combination of speech, signing, pictures, and using actions to convey ASL signs and grammar to learners. This approach apparently tapped into all the language perceptual schemas that learners favored. Students who processed ASL via auditory means preferred lessons involving speaking and looking at print material. Students who processed ASL visually preferred lessons involving vision. Yet others who processed ASL kinesthetically preferred lessons involving actions in ASL.

Variations in language perceptual processing schemas preferred by learners with learning disabilities were similar to those of learners without learning disabilities. This finding agrees with Sparks' (2006, 2009) argument that there was no such a thing as a disability in the learning of foreign languages. Learners with learning disabilities performed similarly to learners who were poor readers. This similarity occurred because learners in the two groups were poor language learners. Foreign language learning problems show a continuum of good to poor language learners (processors) and, therefore, according to Sparks, there is no such a thing as "Foreign Language Learning Disability" (FLLD).

There is no study on the relationship between learning strategy and performance by learners with learning disabilities in foreign language classes. This study found that there was a wide range of correlations between language learning strategy and learner course grade performance. Findings in this study show individual differences in how these learners processed ASL as a second language.

Comparisons of Achievement Correlates between General Education Learners and Learners with Learning Disabilities

Both similarities and differences were found between general education learners and learners with learning disabilities in the relationship between thinking, learning strategies, and course achievement. Variations in thinking and learning strategies were found between learner participants regardless of whether or not they had a learning disability. Both groups of learners achieved high course grades if they noted actions to describe new signs, played ASL language games in class, and asked the teacher if they had questions. A few differences occurred in other correlates between the two groups also. General education learners with high course grades preferred to have English spoken in the classroom, preferred doing project work, and they tended to emphasize vocabulary and grammar as ways of learning ASL. Learners with learning disabilities with high course grades did not translate from ASL to English. These findings suggest that variations in learners with and without learning disability should factor into pedagogical development.

Implications for Pedagogy

The variations among learners with and without learning disabilities in their preferred learning strategies that are associated with higher course grades suggest that teachers should provide differentiated instruction. Differentiated instruction for ASL course learners would ensure that teachers best match their learners to their motivations, language

CHAPTER 5

perceptual processing schemas, and learning strategies that will generate higher course grades. All study learners can hear and speak. However, it cannot be assumed that they were equally motivated to learn ASL and were all auditory processors of linguistic information. As discussed, learners varied in their reasons for taking ASL and in their perceptual processing of the language. This had consequences for their learning of ASL. In order to provide differentiated instruction to learners, teachers need to know what learning strategies learners use for learning the language and why their learners prefer certain strategies over others.

ASL teachers first need to know learners' motivations for learning ASL so they can make learning ASL and about the Deaf community appealing to potential ASL learners. Teachers also need to find out how learners process ASL as a language in order to construct instructional strategies for optimal learner learning. Their instructional strategies may need to accommodate different learner learning strategies, grounded on differing learner motivations and ways of processing language. In essence, teachers need to match instruction to learners' interests and perceptual strengths (Dunn, 1983). While ASL is a visual-manual language, the L2 learners' processing of ASL in the study was shown as related to their preferred perceptual processing schemas.

This implies that for learners preferring the visual modality for learning ASL, teachers may need to use instructional strategies in ways that these learners can match signs with visual representations, such as pictures and videos, of concepts including ideas, entities, and events. Also, for learners preferring the auditory modality for learning ASL, teachers may need to use instructional strategies that will enable learners to use auditory means, such as spoken and written English, to correspond signs with related concepts. In addition, ASL teachers may need to go one step further for these learners. They may have to help them transition gradually from reliance on learning via auditory means to more reliance on vision for processing and learning ASL. It is hoped that this study's results regarding learners' preferences for certain learning strategies will aid teachers in pedagogical planning.

The study results may help ASL teachers in developing better instructional strategies and materials. The correlations discerned in this study were grounded on the content- and task-based communication approach employed by the learners' teachers. Under the approach, ASL teachers taught topics pertaining to daily life and Deaf community and culture, introduced ASL signs and grammar through pictures, actions and words, and constructed conversational tasks for the learners to develop skills in using ASL signs, and grammar to talk about the topics. Learners would then practice and have conversations with each other in signs and ASL sentences learned. The learning activities listed in this study were employed. As described previously, learners' course grades were a compendium of learners' performance in receptive, expressive, and dialogue examinations, homework, projects, presentations, and attendance.

There are motivation, language perceptual processing schemas, and learning strategy contributors of higher learner course grade scores that were found in common across schools. While ASL teachers from the three schools used similar pedagogical approaches in teaching ASL, this study's results imply that certain pedagogical practices were more conducive to higher learner course grades. Also, information from the study about learners' motivations and learning strategies that were conducive to higher learner performance may assist teachers in constructing classroom materials and activities. It is hoped that common contributors to high learner course grades across schools will become materials and strategies for teachers to use in ensuring higher, rather than lower, learner course grades. The following are pedagogical suggestions to achieve better learner performance, based on study findings.

This study found that high learner grades were correlated with certain motivation variables. For learners motivated by intellectual interest in ASL and by the uniqueness of ASL as a language, ASL teachers may want to explain the visual nature of ASL as compared with spoken languages to emphasize the visual acuity and manual dexterity needed to create signs and use ASL grammar to represent concepts in ideas, scenes, and events. Learners may then use this information to develop an appreciation of ASL and delve into using their visual and manual abilities in developing ASL skills. In doing so, ASL teachers challenge learners to learn the intricacies of the visual modality of ASL. Some learners found ASL easier to learn than spoken foreign languages.

Other learners take ASL because they want to learn about deaf people, want to work with deaf people, and want to become ASL teachers as part of their career plans. To appeal to these learners, ASL teachers should develop units on D/HH people and their language, community, and culture in their classrooms. The units should cover topics that pertain to communication and language, education, home life, social experiences, history, community, culture, technology, and employment

It was found that learners who took ASL because of not doing well in other, albeit spoken, foreign languages tended to receive lower course grades. ASL teachers may want to identify these learners' strengths and weaknesses in their learning of other foreign languages and construct instructional plans that tap into their strengths for better success.

To ensure high learner performance in class, ASL teachers should encourage learners to take notes of actions as related to signs learned and have the learners ask them if they have questions. They may want to construct activities, including games, for learners to use and develop ASL skills with each other. ASL teachers need to stress learning ASL vocabulary and grammar to learners because this study found that focus on these areas was conducive to higher learner performance. ASL teachers should try to avoid speaking English in classrooms so learners do not perform poorly. Spoken English, while helpful to some learners, may lead to the danger of learners using it for constructing signs and grammar that are not ASL, but rather are more like those of Signed English or other Manually Coded English systems.

The study found that other learning activities that did not significantly contribute to learner grades, but did shape learners' progress toward higher course grades. ASL teachers should continue doing learning activities that tend to lead to higher learner grades and, if taken in combination, may contribute to learners' high course achievement. Teachers should keep on using only ASL as the classroom language and continue encouraging learners to take notes in pictures and/or in English words to help them remember signs. ASL teachers should plan activities, such giving narrations, doing dialogues, doing grammar exercises, and emphasizing learning discourse. The teachers should encourage their students to ask them questions and to look up needed information in the course textbook, dictionary, the Internet, CDs, or videos. As described in the methods section, these learning activities are multimodality in nature and are useful for learners who use different language processing schemas. Textbooks, homework, projects, and games provide both visual and print medium. Other activities such as employing narration and dialogues in class and learners doing homework and/or projects are activities that tap into learners' different perceptual processing schemas and take into account their preferred language perceptual processing schemas. Teachers should tap into their learners' motivation for taking ASL, language perceptual processing strengths, and incorporate learners' learning strategies so they can master ASL and have high achievement levels.

Based on this study's results on the relationship between learner grades and other learning strategies, certain learning activities were found to be detrimental to learners' performance in ASL. ASL teachers should avoid, or minimize, using a combination of spoken English and ASL in classrooms, relying on learners' textbooks to teach lessons, and having learners translate from English to ASL. They should also discourage learners from thinking of English words and sentences when learning ASL.

6

Conclusion

Similarities in findings between this study and previous studies, if any, would attest to universal principles of language learning, in general, and learning foreign languages, in particular. Any differences would attest to the unique process of learning ASL as a foreign language.

One study finding was that motivation was a function of personal reasons for using the language and for social participation. Motivation and language perceptual processing schema were found to shape learning strategies that learners used for learning ASL. In turn, learners' motivations and language learning strategies used were found to influence learner course achievement. General education learners used similar language perceptual processing schemas and learning strategies that learners with learning disabilities employed. Since this study looked at how learners with and without learning disabilities learned ASL as a second language, it is necessary to compare results of both learner groups to assess similarities and differences between them.

Statistical analyses were employed that revealed groups of learner language perceptual processing schemas. General education learners tended to think in pictures, think in actions for describing ASL signs, and to think in terms of English translation. It was revealed that learners with learning disabilities used two language perceptual processing schemas, namely, thinking in pictures and in terms of English translation.

Correlations were conducted regarding learners' learning strategies. Students with and without learning disabilities diverged widely in terms of learners' preferred learning strategies in ASL classes. The general education learners who thought in actions and in English translations relied on L1 English words to learn ASL signs and relied on L1 English sentences to learn ASL signs. The only function to significantly correlate with reliance on L1 English words when learning new ASL

CONCLUSION

signs for learners with learning disabilities was thinking in English translation.

Learners without learning disabilities who thought in pictures and actions took notes in picture format as a means of learning ASL signs, while learners without learning disabilities who thought in terms of actions and English translation did not take notes in pictures and sign formats. The thinking in pictures function was the only significant correlate for learners with learning disabilities' note-taking strategy of drawing in pictures.

Students without learning disabilities who thought in terms of actions and English translations, but not in a combination of pictures and actions, preferred that their teachers use both spoken English and ASL in class. Only the thinking in English translation function significantly correlated with students with learning disabilities' preference to have both ASL and spoken English, but not solely English, used in class. Students who thought in English translations and in a combination of pictures and actions, but not of actions alone, emphasized learning ASL vocabulary, grammar, and discourse in ASL classes. The thinking in English translation function significantly correlated with learners' emphasis on learning grammar in ASL class for learners with learning disabilities.

Only three language learning strategies did not significantly differ for learners without learning disabilities. These included learners following textbooks, watching classroom activities, and doing homework as ways for learning ASL.

For learners with learning disabilities, other learning strategies that pertain to learning activities and getting answers to questions were not significantly correlated with any of the learning strategies. The learning strategies they most often used were taking notes of signs, using L1 English to learn ASL, and the linguistic area of ASL they emphasized for study in learning the language.

However, several significant differences existed among clusters in other language learning strategies that learners preferred. LSD post-hoc tests were performed to assess which clusters significantly differed from others for each of the questionnaire items about language learning strategies.

A few significant correlations were seen between preferred learning strategies and higher learner course grades. Learners without learning disabilities who earned higher grades significantly correlated with the learning activities of playing ASL games in class, doing project work, asking teachers their questions, and emphasizing vocabulary and grammar as the preferred linguistic areas on which to concentrate for learning ASL. The students with learning disabilities who achieved higher grades took notes in actions while learning new ASL signs, played language games in class, asked teachers their questions, and did not translate from ASL to English.

However, learners without learning disabilities received lower course grades if they used the note-taking strategy of putting down actions to describe new signs and if as much English as possible was spoken in class. These factors both correlated negatively and significantly with lower learner grades. Other language learning strategy variables were not significantly correlated with course grades for both learners with and without learning disabilities.

These study results have several implications regarding hearing high school learners' learning of ASL. The implications involve how hearing learners process ASL as a language and their use of ASL to help them in mastering cognitive and literacy skills.

Brain studies have demonstrated how the brain processes visual, auditory, and tactile information. Several studies have consistently shown that individuals vary in their preferred modalities for coding and processing information (McDonald et al., 2001). This is true regardless of their sensory-based abilities to process languages and the modality of a given language. While each sense modality organizes space and sensory information in particular ways (De Renzi et al., 1970), there is transfer of one sense to another sense modality (Teder-Sälejärvi et al., 1999), interaction between senses (Shimojo & Shams, 2001; Teder-Sälejärvi et al., 2002), and modifications within senses in the sensory processing of information (e.g., Shams, 2002).

These studies demonstrated that a disconnect exists between sensory ability for receiving information and sensory processing of information. This means that, for instance, there is no relationship between hearing ability and preferred sensory modality; the ability to hear does not

Conclusion

automatically translate into a preference for aural-oral modality in processing language. Since ASL is visual, it provides hearing learners who prefer to process information in the visual coding schemata with the opportunity to visualize concepts associated with signs, particularly those that involve spatial reasoning connected with spatial arrangements and directions of entities and actions.

The fact some learners took ASL to develop better visual acuity suggests that ASL is useful in helping learners develop cognitive skills in spatial reasoning. ASL learners learned in class how deaf and hard of hearing individuals orient to spaces in their interactions and within architectures. Studies in DeafSpace have explored how the visual orientation of signing deaf and hard of hearing individuals necessitates alterations in the architectures and arrangements of objects within architectural structures (Hott, 2007; Bauman, 2009; Rains, 2011). Learners learned how deaf and hard of hearing individuals construct and rearrange architectural structures and objects to maximize fields of vision in ASL course units on Deaf culture. In using this information, L2 ASL learners learned how to use space for communication with other signers. L2 learners, in learning about how D/HH people use space, gained an alternate means of signing concepts and conceptualizing signs; understood how to use space for communication purposes, and how to use signs to mark spatial relations. In this way, learners developed an appreciation of the spatial orientations of deaf and hard of hearing individuals. ASL classes provided learners with sign-concept representations with which they were able to produce conceptually correct, both lexically and grammatically, linguistic information instead of creating sign-phonological representations that oralists and those using Signed English methods favor for learners who have difficulties processing information via auditory means.

For learners who took ASL to help develop English literacy skills, ASL provided them with a conceptual framework that helped them process and produce lexical and grammatical information in English. There are studies, particularly with children who are deaf and hard of hearing, and children who can speak and hear but experience learning disabilities, that attest to the utility of ASL for English literacy development. The studies showed that ASL helps enhance learners' mastery of English, particularly for learners who do not have learning disabilities (Daniels, 1993, 1994, 1996, 2001; Towell, 1998) and learners with learning disabilities (Poulton & Algozzine, 1980; Berescik, 1989; McKnight, 1979; Vernon et al., 1980; Greenberg et al., 1982; Hafer 1985; Mandel, 1991). Further exploration of the use of signed languages in helping learners process spoken languages is an area for future research.

However, even if this study's survey results utilized some of the original or modified forms of the *AMTB* and *BALLI,* learner-participants' questionnaire responses cannot be generalized to other learners taking other foreign languages either within participating study schools or in other schools. The study results were appliable only to learner respondents from the five schools. Learners' responses in this study should be interpreted with this caveat.

Pedagogical Implications for ASL Classes Containing Learners With and Without Learning Disabilities

Here, suggestions for pedagogy are provided for teachers who teach ASL to learners with and without disabilities. This study suggests several implications for teaching ASL so all learners can achieve optimal learning, regardless if they have a learning disability or not. Teachers should begin by recognizing that learners employ different thinking strategies, or language perceptual processing of ASL, in learning ASL as a second language. The varying preferred perceptual processing modes learners used, in turn, predicted the activities that they preferred doing when learning ASL, which had consequences for their course performance.

For example, learners in lower level ASL classes exhibited both visually-based and auditorially-based language perceptual processing schemas, that is, processing ASL both in terms of pictures and actions, and in its English translation, and learners in higher level ASL classes exhibited largely visually-based language processing schema, processing ASL in terms of pictures and actions. Higher learner grades were found to associate with teachers' use of both ASL and spoken English in lower level ASL classes. When teachers used only ASL in higher level classes, this was associated with higher learner course grades. Depending on learners' preferred modality for processing ASL at different course levels,

CONCLUSION

exclusive use of either target or native language may generate lower course grades for some learners at lower course levels and, by contrast, heavy use of the target language at higher course levels may generate higher learner course grades.

These findings imply that teachers alternate between the use of target language and native language when teaching ASL. The target language in ASL classes, obviously, is ASL, and the native language is spoken or printed English. The use of target language in ASL classes is associated with teachers using pictures and actions, without using their voices, when introducing signs. By contrast, the use of the native language, English, in ASL classes means that teachers use English gloss and their voices when teaching signs. The aim of ASL learning is so that second language learners can sign like native ASL users, that is, people who do not use their voice and, instead, use visual imagery to express conversational concepts. When introducing new concepts, teachers should begin by showing pictures and introducing signs without using their voices. They should anticipate that some learners will understand, and others will not. Teachers should then repeat the process for learners who do not understand, by using English gloss corresponding to signs, first without voice, and then with voice. Also, in lower ASL level classes, teachers should alternate between using target and native languages. Conversely, in higher level ASL classes, they should use mostly the target language when teaching ASL.

Teachers should initially encourage learners to take notes about ASL signs in any way they feel comfortable in using. As the learners develop ASL skills, teachers should encourage them to take notes either in terms of actions or in picture format, since these note-taking forms have been found as contributing to higher learner grades. They should also discourage the use of English gloss, since that tends to contribute to lower learner grades.

Teachers should construct a multi-battery of instructional materials and strategies for all learners since it was shown in the study that learners used different ways for mastering ASL and preferred certain activities for learning ASL. By doing this, learners will be given the opportunity to master ASL in ways that best benefit them according to how they prefer to process the language.

CHAPTER 6

Implications for Future Research

Future research directions are suggested by the study. First, study results were based on learners' self-reports of their perception and learning strategies, which may or may not reflect their actual classroom work. What needs to be studied is how the learners operationalize their perception and learning strategies for higher achievement in their actual classroom work. Second, only five high schools in a specified location, viz., New York City and its vicinity, were study sites. Learners in other schools and U.S. regions might have different perceptions of the language and strategies for learning it. Third, it is also not known how learner motivation is related to their beliefs about ASL and how beliefs shape their strategies for learning ASL and influence their achievement. Pedagogy for higher learner achievement may be furthered informed by studying and understanding the relationship between learner beliefs, learning strategies for learning ASL, and course achievement.

REFERENCES

American Council for the Teaching of Foreign Languages, Inc. (1993). National standards in foreign language learning. Washington, DC: Author.

American Council for the Teaching of Foreign Languages, Inc. (1999). American standards for foreign language learning in the 21st century. Alexandra, VA: Author.

Anderson, J. R. (1983). *The architecture of cognition.* Cambridge: Harvard University Press.

Anderson, J. R. (1985). *Cognitive psychology and its implications.* (2nd ed.). New York: Freeman.

Antia, S. D., Stinson, M. S., & Gaustad, M. G. (2002). Developing membership in the education of deaf and hard of hearing in inclusive settings. *Journal of Deaf Studies and Deaf Education,* 7: 214–228.

Armstrong, D. F. (1988). Some notes on ASL as a "foreign" language. *Sign Language Studies,* 59: 231–239.

Baker, S. C., & MacIntyre, P. D. (2003). The role of gender and immersion in communication and second language orientations. In Z. Dörnyei, (Ed.), *Attitudes, orientations, and motivations in language learning: Advances in theory, research, and applications* (pp. 65–96). Malden, MA: Blackwell Publishing.

Baker-Schenk, C., & Cokely, D. (1980). *Green Books: American Sign Language teacher's resource text on curriculum, methods and evaluation.* Washington, DC: Gallaudet University Press.

Barbe, W. B., & Swassing, R. H. (1979). *Teaching through modality strengths: Concept and practices.* Columbus, OH: Zaner-Bloser.

Barrera, M. (2003). Curriculum-based dynamic assessment for new- or second-language learners with learning disabilities in high education settings. *Assessment for Effective Intervention,* 29(1): 69–84.

Battison, R., & Carter, S. M. (1981). The academic status of sign language. In F. Caccamise, M. Garretson, & U. Bellugi (Eds.), *Teaching American Sign Language as a second/foreign language* (pp. v–xiii). Silver Spring, MD: National Association of the Deaf.

Bauman, H.-D. (2009). Deaf diverse design guide: Identifying the principles of deaf space. Retrieved from www.dangermondarchitects.com/blog/?page_id+13, April 5, 2010.

REFERENCES

Baynton, D. (1996). *Forbidden signs: American culture and the campaign against sign language*. Chicago, IL: University of Chicago Press.

Belka, R. W. (2000). Is American Sign Language a "foreign" language? *NECTFL Review*, 48: 45–52.

Belmechri, F., & Hummel, K. (1998). Orientations and motivation in the acquisition of English as a second language among high school students in Quebec City. *Language Learning*, 48: 219–244.

Berescik, S. J. (1989). To learn in a different style: An LD success story. *Academic Therapy*, 24(3): 289–93.

Caccamise, F., Garretson, M., & Bellugi, U. (1981). *Teaching American Sign Language as a second/foreign language*. Silver Spring, MD: National Association of the Deaf.

California Department of Education. (2006a). *Course enrollments by subject*. Sacramento, CA: California Department of Education, Educational Demographics Unit.

California Department of Education. (2006b). *Number of teachers by subject*. Sacramento, CA: California Department of Education, Educational Demographics Unit.

Center for Applied Linguistics. (1997). *A national survey of foreign language instruction in elementary and high schools: A changing picture: 1987–1997*. Washington, DC: Author.

Chamot, A. U., Kupper, L., & Impink-Hernandez, M. V. (1988a). *A study of learning strategies in foreign language instruction: Findings from a longitudinal study*. Arlington, VA: Interstate Research Associates.

Chamot, A. U., Kupper, L., & Impink-Hernandez, M. V. (1988b). *A study of learning strategies in foreign language instruction: The third year and final report*. McLean, VA: Interstate Research Associates.

Chang, S. F., & Huang, S. C. (1999). *Language learning motivation and language learning strategies of Taiwanese EFL students*. Technical Report. ERIC ED428561.

Charlson, E., Strong, M., & Gold, R. (1992). How successful deaf teenagers experience and cope with isolation. *American Annals of the Deaf*, 137: 261–270.

Chen, A. (2009). Perception of paralinguistic intonational meaning in a second language. *Language Learning*, 59(2): 367–409.

Chen, Y.-C. (2008). Vocabulary learning strategies to improve EFL students' comprehension of reading in a foreign language in Taiwan (China). *Dissertation Abstracts International: Section A. Humanities and Social Sciences*, 68(7-A), 2769.

Chen, Y.-L. (1999). *Motivation and language learning strategies in learning English as a foreign language*. (Unpublished doctoral dissertation). The University of Washington, Seattle, WA.

Chiang, H.-H. (2005). The relationship between field sensitivity/field independence and the use of vocabulary learning strategies of EFL university students in Taiwan (China). *Dissertation Abstracts International: Section A. Humanities and Social Sciences*, 65(8-A), 2868.

REFERENCES

Chopin, P. (1988). American Sign Language and the liberal education. *Sign Language Studies*, 59: 109–115.

Chou, Y.-C. (2002). *An exploratory study of language learning strategies and the relationship of these strategies to motivation and language proficiency among EFL Taiwanese technological and vocational college students.* (Unpublished doctoral dissertation). The University of Iowa, Iowa City, IA.

Chuang, Y. (2004). The National English Test in Proficiency for All on the Web in Taiwan (NETPAW). Retrieved from http://www.atriumlinguarum.org/contenido/13ok-O%5C'Neill.pdf, September 5, 2011.

Clary, W. M., Jr. (2004). *American Sign Language as high school language elective: Factors influencing its adoption.* (Doctoral dissertation). University of Southern California (University Microfiche International No. 3145184).

Clement, R., & Kruidenier, C. B. (1985). Aptitude, attitude and motivation in second language proficiency: A test of Clement's model. Journal of Language and Social Psychology, 4: 21–37.

Cochran-Smith, M., & Lytle, S. L. (1993). *Inside outside: Teacher research and knowledge.* New York: Teachers College Press.

Commission on Education of the Deaf. (1988). *Toward equality: Education of the deaf.* Washington, DC: U.S. Government Printing Office.

Cooper, S. B. (1997). *The academic status of sign language programs in institutions of higher education in the United States.* (Unpublished doctoral dissertation). Gallaudet University, Washington, D.C.

Corwin, K., & Wilcox, S. (1985). The search for the empty cup continues. *Sign Language Studies*, 48: 249–268.

Critchley, M. (1964). *Development dyslexia.* Springfield, IL: Charles C. Thomas.

Crookes, G., & Schmidt, R.W. (1991). Motivation: Reopening the research agenda. *Language Learning*, 33: 272–291.

Csizer, K., & Dörnyei, Z. (2005). The internal structure of language learning motivation and its relationship with language choice and learning effort. *The Modern Language Journal*, 89(1): 19–36.

Daniels, M. (1993). ASL as a factor in acquiring English. *Sign Language Studies*, 78: 23–29.

Daniels, M. (1994). The effect of sign language on hearing children's language development. *Communication Education*, 43: 291–298.

Daniels, M. (1996). The effect over time of sign language on vocabulary development in early childhood education. *Child Study Journal*, 26(3): 193–208.

Daniels, M. (2001). *Dancing with words: Signing for hearing children's literacy.* Westport, CT: Bergin & Garvey.

Davis, L. (1998). The linguistic turf battles over American Sign Language. *The Chronicle of Higher Education*, 44: 60–64.

DeFino, S. M., & Lombardino, L. J. (2004). Language learning disabilities: The ultimate foreign language challenge. *Foreign language Annals*, 37(3): 390–400.

REFERENCES

De Renzi E., Faglioni, P., & Scotti, G. (1970). Hemispheric contribution to exploration of space through the visual and tactile modality. *Cortex*, 6: 191–203.

Devine, J. (1988). A case study of two readers: Models of reading and reading performance. In P. L. Carrell, J. Devine, & D. Eskey (Eds.), *Interactive approaches to second language reading* (pp. 127–139). Cambridge: Cambridge University Press.

Dinklage, K. T. (1971). Inability to learn a foreign language. In G. Blaine, & C. McArthur (Eds.), *Emotional problems of the student* (pp. 185–206). New York: Appleton-Century-Crofts.

Dörnyei, Z. (2001). *Teaching and researching motivation*. Harlow, UK: Longman.

Dörnyei, Z. (2003). Attitudes, orientations, and motivations in language learning: Advances in theory, research, and applications. In Z. Dörnyei (Ed.), *Attitudes, orientations, and motivations in language learning: Advances in theory, research, and applications* (pp. 3–32). Malden, MA: Blackwell Publishing.

Dörnyei, Z. (2005). *The psychology of he language learner: Individual differences in second language acquisition*. Mahwah, NJ: Lawrence Erlbaum.

Dörnyei, Z., & Clement, R. (2001). Motivational characteristics of learning different target languages: Results of a nationwide survey. In Z. Dörnyei, & R. Schmidt, (Eds.), *Motivation and second language acquisition* (Tech. Rep. No. 23, pp. 399–432). Honolulu, HI: University of Hawai'i at Manoa, Second Language Teaching and Curriculum Center.

Dörnyei, Z., & Csizer, K. (2002). Some dynamics of language attitudes and motivation: Results of a longitudinal nationwide survey. *Applied Linguistics*, 23: 421–462.

Dörnyei, Z., & Ushioda, E, (Eds.). (2009). *Motivation, language identity and the L2 self*. Bristol, UK: Multilingual Matters.

Dounay, J. (2002). *Foreign language requirements for high school graduation*. Washington, DC: Education Commission of the States.

Dreyer, C., & Oxford, R. I. (1996). Learning strategies and other predictors of ESL proficiency among Afrikaans speakers in South Africa. In R. L. Oxford, (Ed.), *Language learning strategies around the world: Cross-cultural perspectives* (pp. 61–74). Manoa: University of Hawai'i Press.

Dunn, R. (1983). Learning style and its relation to exceptionality at both ends of the spectrum. *Exceptional Children*, 49: 496–506.

Dunn, R. S., &. Dunn, K. J. (1979). Learning styles/teaching styles: Should they . . . can they . . . be matched? *Educational Leadership*, 36: 238–244.

Education for All Handicapped Children Act. Pub. L. No. 94–142, 89 Stat. 773 (1975).

Ely, C. M. (1986). Language learning motivation: A descriptive causal analysis. *Modern Language Journal*, 70: 28–35.

Feenstra, H. J. (2006). Aptitude, attitude, and motivation in second-language acquisition. *Dissertation Abstracts International: Section B. Sciences and Engineering*, 67(1-B): 570.

Field, A. (2005). *Discovering statistics using SPSS*. (2nd ed.). London: Sage.

REFERENCES

Final Regulations for Part B of the Individuals with Disabilities Education Act, 34 C.F.R. Part 300. (1999).

Fischer, S., & Siple, P. (1990). *Theoretical issues in sign language research*. Chicago: University of Chicago Press.

Flemens, K. (2009). *Motivation, language-learning strategies, and course performance among English-speaking college students learning a romance language*. (Unpublished doctoral dissertation). Lynn University, Boca Raton, FL.

Foster, S. (1989). Social alienation and peer identification: A study of the social construction of deafness. *Human Organization*, 48: 226–235.

Frishberg, N. (1988). Signers of tales: The case for literary status of an unwritten language. *Sign Language Studies*, 59: 149–170.

Fromkin, V. A. (1988). Sign language: Evidence for language universals and the linguistic capacity of the human brain. *Sign Language Studies*, 59: 115–128.

Gallaudet Research Institute. (2004a). *Regional and national summary report of data from the annual survey of deaf and hard of hearing children and youth*. Washington, DC: GRI: Gallaudet University.

Gallaudet Research Institute. (2004b). *States that recognize American Sign language as a foreign language*. Retrieved from http://clerccenter.gallaudet.edu/InfoToGo/index.html, July 10, 2006.

Gannon, J. (1981). *Deaf heritage: A narrative history of Deaf America*. Silver Spring, MD: National Association of the Deaf.

Ganschow, L, & Sparks, R. 2000. Reflections on foreign language study for students with language learning problems: Research, issues and challenges. *Dyslexia*, 6: 87–100.

Ganschow, L., Sparks, R. L., & Javorsky, J. (1998). Foreign language learning difficulties: An historical perspective. *Journal of Learning Disabilities*, 31(3): 248–258.

Gardner, R. C. (1985). *Social psychology and second language learning: The role of attitudes and motivation*. London: Edward Arnold.

Gardner, R. C. (2001). Integrative motivation and second language acquisition. In Z. Dörnyei, & R. Schmidt, (Eds.), *Motivation and second language learning*, (pp. 1–19). Honolulu, HI: University of Hawai'i Press.

Gardner, R. C. (2006). The socio-educational model of second language acquisition: A research paradigm. In S. H. Foster-Cohen, M. M. Krajnovic, & J. M. Djigunovic, (Eds.), *EUROSLA yearbook: Annual Conference of the European Second Language Association, Volume 6* (pp. 237–260). Amsterdam: Johns Benjamins.

Gardner, R. C., Lalonde, R. N., & Moorcroft, R. (1985). The role of attitudes and motivation in second language learning: Correlational and experimental considerations. *Language Learning*, 35(2): 207–227.

Gardner, R. C., & Lambert, W. E. (1959). Motivational variables in second language acquisition. *Canadian Journal of Psychology*, 13: 266–272.

Gardner, R. C., & MacIntyre, P. D. (1993). On the measurement of affective variables in second language learning. *Language Learning*, 43: 157–194.

REFERENCES

Gardner, R. C., Masgoret, A.-M., Tennant, J., & Mihic, L. (2004). Integrative motivation: Changes during a year-long intermediate-level language course. *Language Learning*, 54: 1–34.

Gardner, R. C., & Smythe, P. C. (1975). Motivation and second language acquisition. *Canadian Modern Language Review*, 31: 218–230.

Gardner, R. C., Tremblay, P. E., & Masgoret, A.-M. (1997). Towards a full model of second language learning: An empirical investigation. *Modern Language Journal*, 81: 344–362.

Garner, R., & Alexander, P. A. (Eds.). (1994). *Beliefs about text and instruction with text*. Hillsdale, NJ: Lawrence Erlbaum Associates.

Garner, R., & Hansis, R. (1994). Literacy practices outside of school: Adolescent beliefs and their responses to "street texts." In R. Garner & P. A. Alexander, (Eds.), *Beliefs about text and instruction with text* (pp. 57–73). Hillsdale, NJ: Lawrence Erlbaum Associates.

Gaustad, M. G., & Kluwin, T. N. (1992). Patterns of communication among deaf and hearing adolescents. In T. N. Kluwin, D. F. Moores, & M. G. Gaustad (Eds.), *Toward effective school programs for deaf students* (pp. 107–128). New York: Teachers College Press.

Ghenghesh, P. (2010). The motivation of learners of Arabic: Does it decrease with age? *Journal of Language Teaching and Research*, 1(3): 235–249.

Goodman, J., Freed, B., & McMannus, W. J. (1988). The measurement of foreign language learning disabilities in college students. *Journal of Learning Disabilities*, 21(7): 429–430.

Greenberg, J. C., Vernon, M., DuBois, J. H., & McKnight, J. C. (1982). *The language arts handbook: A total communication approach*. Baltimore: University Park Press.

Grosse, C. U., Tuman, W. V., & Critz, M. A. (1998). The economic utility of foreign language study. *Modern Language Journal*, 82(4): 457–472.

Hafer, J. C. (1985). The effect of signing as a multisensory technique for teaching sight vocabulary to learning disabled hearing students. *Dissertation Abstracts International: Section A. Humanities and Social Sciences, Dissertation Abstracts International*, 46(6-A): 1577.

Horwitz, E. K. (1988). The beliefs about language learning of beginning university foreign language students. *Modern Language Journal*, 72: 283–294.

Horwitz, R. (1994). Adolescent beliefs about oral and written language. In R. Garner & P. A. Alexander (Eds.), *Beliefs about text and instruction with text* (pp. 1–24). Hillsdale, NJ: Lawrence Erlbaum Associates.

Hott, L. (2007). *Through Deaf eyes: A photographic history of an American Community*. Washington, DC: WETA and Florentine Films/Hott Productions.

Hou, Y-A. (2009). *An investigation of perceptual learning style preferences, language learning strategy use, and English achievement: A case study of Taiwanese EFL learners*. (Unpublished doctoral dissertation). La Sierra University, Riverside, CA.

Humphries, T., & Padden, C. (1992). *Learning American Sign Language, Levels I and II—Beginning and Intermediate*. Boston: Pearson Education, Inc.

REFERENCES

Indiana Department of Education. (2006a). *Trends in foreign language enrollment in Indiana.* Indianapolis, IN: Indiana Department of Education, Indiana Accountability System for Academic Progress. Retrieved from www.doe.state.in.U.S./opd/wrldlangs/ET_04-05.doc., July 10, 2006.

Indiana Department of Education. (2006b). *Number of teachers by subject.* Indianapolis, IN: Indiana Department of Education, Indiana Accountability System for Academic Progress. Retrieved from www.doe.state.in.U.S./opd/wrldlangs/ET_04-05.doc., July 10, 2006.

Individuals with Disabilities Education Act. (1997). 20 U.S.C. Section 1400–1487. (Supp. III).

Jacobowitz, E. L. (1996). President's report. *ASLTA Quarterly* 2: 1.

Jacobowitz, E. L. (1999, October). *American Sign Language in higher education: Implications for administrators and teacher trainers.* Presented at American Sign Language Teachers Association Professional Development Conference, Rochester, NY.

Javorsky, J., Sparks, R., &. Ganschow, L. (1992). Perceptions of college students with and without specific learning disabilities about foreign language courses. *Learning Disabilities Research and Practice,* 7: 31–44.

Kanda, J., & Fleischer, L. (1988). Who is qualified to teach American Sign Language? *Sign Language Studies,* 59: 183–194.

Kang, S. (2000). Modeling relationships between the use of English as a second language learning strategies and the test performance of Asian students. *Dissertation Abstracts International Section A: Humanities and Social Sciences.* 60(9-A): 3295.

Kaylani, C. T. (1995). *The influence of gender and motivation on the language learning strategy use of successful and unsuccessful English language students in Jordan* (Unpublished doctoral dissertation). The University of Pittsburgh, Pittsburgh, PA.

Keefe, J. W. (1979). Learning style: An overview. In J. W. Keefe, (Ed.), *Student learning styles: Diagnosing and prescribing programs* (pp. 1–17). Reston VA: National Association of High School Principals.

Keefe, J. W. (1987). *Learning style: theory and practice.* Reston, VA: National Association of High School Principals.

Kemp, M. (1989). An acculturation model for learners of ASL. In C. Lucas, (Ed.), *Sociolinguistics in Deaf communities,* Vol. 4 (pp. 213–230). Washington, DC: Gallaudet University Press.

Kemp, M. (1998). Why is learning American Sign language a challenge? *American Annals of the Deaf,* 143(3): 255–259.

Kiger, G. (1997). The structure of attitudes toward persons who are deaf: Emotions, values, and stereotypes. *Journal of Psychology,* 131: 554–560.

Kinsella, K. (1995). Perceptual Learning Preferences Survey. In J. M. Reid, (Ed.), *Learning styles in the ESL/EFL classroom* (pp. 221–235). Boston: Heinle and Heinle.

Kissau, S. (2006). Gender differences in motivation to learn French. *Canadian Modern Language Review,* 62(3): 401–422.

REFERENCES

Klima, E., & Bellugi, U. (1979). *The signs of language*. Cambridge, MA: Harvard University Press.

Kormos, J., & Csizer, K. (2008). Age-related differences in the motivation of learning English as a foreign language: Attitudes, selves and motivated learning behavior. *Language Learning*, 58(2): 327–355.

Kreeft-Peyton, J. (1998). ASL as a foreign language. *K-12 Foreign Language Education*, 6: 1–3.

Kroonenberg, N. (1995). Meeting language learners' sensory-learning style. In J. M. Reid, (Ed.), *Learning styles in the ESL/EFL classroom* (pp. 74–86). Boston: Heinle and Heinle.

Lalonde, R. N., & Gardner, R. C. (1985). On the predictive validity of the Attitude/Motivation Test Battery. *Journal of Multilingual and Multicultural Development*, 6: 403–412.

Lane, H. (1984). *When the mind hears: A history of the deaf*. New York: Random House.

Lane, H., Hoffmeister, R., & Bahan, B. (1996). *A journey into the Deaf-World*. San Diego, CA: DawnSignPress.

Lang, H. G., Foster, S., Gustina, D., Mowl, G., & Lui, Y. (1996). Motivational and attitudinal orientations in learning American Sign Language. *Journal of Deaf Studies and Deaf Education*, 1(2): 137–144.

Lee, C., & Anita, S. (1992). A sociological approach to the social integration of hearing impaired and normally hearing students. *Volta Review*, 95: 425–434.

Letteri, C. A. (1988). The NASSP Learning Style Profile and cognitive processing. In J. W. Keefe (Ed.), *Profiling and utilizing learning style* (pp. 22–34). Reston, VA: National Association of High School Principals.

Liddell, S. K. (1980). *American Sign Language syntax*. The Hague: Mouton Publishers.

Loux, D. (1996). *Report of the legislative task force on American Sign Language to the members of the 69th session of the Nevada Legislature*. Nevada (booklet). Cited in Pfeffier, D., op. cit.

Lukmani, Y. M. (1972). Motivation to learn and language proficiency. *Language Learning*, 22(2): 261–273.

Mabbott, A. (1994). An exploration of reading comprehension, oral reading errors, and written errors by subjects labeled learning disabled. *Foreign Language Annals*, 27: 293–324.

Macaro, E. (2001). *Learning strategies in foreign and second language classrooms*. New York: Continuum.

MacIntyre, P. D., Baker, S. C., Clement, R., & Donovan, L. A. (2003). Sex and age effects on willingness to communicate, anxiety, perceived competence, and L2 motivation among junior high school French immersion students. In Z. Dörnyei, (Ed.), *Attitudes, orientations, and motivations in language learning: Advances in theory, research, and applications* (pp. 137–165). Malden, MA: Blackwell Publishing.

REFERENCES

Mandel, L. A. (1991). The effect of signing key words for demonstrating work instructions to learning-disabled students. *Dissertation Abstracts International: Section A. Humanities and Social Sciences*, 52(4-A): 1275.

Masgoret, A-M., & Gardner, R. C. (2003). Attitudes, motivation, and second language learning: A meta-analysis of studies conducted by Gardner and associates. *Language Learning*, 53 (Suppl 1): 167–210.

Mayberry, R. I., Lock, E., & Kazmi, H. (2002). Development: Linguistic ability and early language exposure. *Nature*, 417: 38.

McDonald, J. J., Teder-Sälejärvi, W. A., & Ward, L. M. (2001). Multisensory integration and cross-modal attention effects in the human brain. *Science*, 292: 1791.

McKee, R. L., & McKee, D. (1992). What's so hard about learning ASL?: Students' and teachers' perceptions. *Sign Language Studies*, 75: 129–157.

McKnight, J. C. (1979). Using the manual alphabet in teaching reading to learning disabled children. *Journal of Learning Disabilities*, 12(9): 581–584.

Miller, L. (1976). *Attitudes toward deafness, motivation and expectations of students enrolled in manual communication classes.* (Unpublished doctoral dissertation). Brigham Young University, Provo, UT.

Minggui, G., & Yu, J. (2005). A study on the relationships between English learning strategies and academic achievements of middle school students. *Psychological Science* (China), 28(2): 451–453.

Mochizuki, A. (1999). Language learning strategies used by Japanese university students. *RELC Journal*, 30(2): 101–113.

Modern Language Association (2010). *Enrollments in languages other than English in United States institutions of higher education, Fall 2009.* (http://www.mla.org/pdf/2009_enrollment_survey.pdf, accessed on March 21, 2015).

Modern Language Association (2015). *Language enrollment database, 1958–2013.* (https://www.mla.org/cgi-shl/docstudio/docs.pl?flsurvey_results, accessed on March 21, 2015).

Moores, D. M. (2001). *Educating the deaf: Psychology, principles and practices.* (5th ed.). New York: Houghton-Mifflin.

Mori, S., & Gobel, P. (2006). Motivation and gender in the Japanese EFL classroom. *System*, 34(2): 194–210.

Mullins, P. Y. (1992). *Successful English language learning strategies of ESL college students.* (Unpublished doctoral dissertation). International University, San Diego, CA.

Naiman, N., Frohlich, M., Stern, H., & Todesco, A. (1978). *The good language learner.* Research in Education Series No. 7. Toronto: Ontario Institute for Studies in Education.

Nakayama, A. (2005). Testing a hypothesized model of English language learning: Japanese university students' goal orientation, beliefs, and learning strategies. *Japanese Journal of Educational Psychology*, 53(3): 320–330.

Nash, J. E. (2000). Shifting stigma from body to self: Paradoxical consequences of mainstreaming. In P. E. Spencer, C .J. Erting, & M. Marshark (Eds.), *The deaf*

REFERENCES

child in the family and at school (pp. 211–227). Mahwah, NJ: Lawrence Erlbaum and Associates.

National Joint Committee on Learning Disabilities. (2000). *Modifications to the NJCLD definition of learning disabilities.* Washington, DC: Author.

Neidle, C., Kegl, J., MacLaughlin, D., Bahan, B., & Lee, R. (2000). *The syntax of American Sign Language: Functional categories and hierarchical structure.* Cambridge, MA: MIT Press.

Newell, W. (1994). *A job analysis of teaching American Sign Language.* Ann Arbor, MI: University Microfilms. No. LD3041.

Newell W. (1995a). A profile of professionals teaching American Sign Language. *Sign Language Studies*, 86: 19–36.

Newell W. (1995b). American Sign Language teachers: Practices and perceptions. *Sign Language Studies*, 87: 141–165.

Nisbet, D. L. (2003). Language learning strategies and English proficiency of Chinese university learners. *Dissertation Abstracts International Section A: Humanities and Social Sciences.* 63 (10-A): 3500.

Nisbet, D. L., Tindall, E. R., & Arroyo, A. A. (2005). Language learning strategies and English proficiency of Chinese university students. *Foreign Language Annals*, 38(1): 100–107.

Noels, K. A. (2001). New orientations in language learning motivation: Towards a model of intrinsic, extrinsic, and integrative orientations and motivation. In Z. Dörnyei, & R. Schmidt, (Eds.), *Motivation and second language acquisition* (Tech. Rep. No. 23 (pp. 43–68). Honolulu, HI: University of Hawai'i at Manoa, Second Language Teaching and Curriculum Center.

Noels, K. A. (2003). Learning Spanish as a second language: Learner's orientations and perceptions of their teachers' communication style. In Z. Dörnyei, (Ed.), *Attitudes, orientations, and motivations in language learning: Advances in theory, research, and applications* (pp. 97–136). Malden, MA: Blackwell Publishing.

Noels, K. A., Pelletier, L. G., Clement, R., & Vallerand, R. J. (2000). Why are you learning a second language? Motivational orientations and self-determination theory. *Language Learning*, 50: 57–85.

Nyikos, M., & Oxford, R. L. (1993). A factor analytic study of language learning strategy use: Interpretations from information-processing theory and social psychology. *Modern Language Journal*, 7: 11–22.

Okada, M., Oxford, R. L., & Abo, S. (1996). Not all alike: Motivation and learning strategies among students of Japanese and Spanish: An exploratory study. In R. L. Oxford, (Ed.), *Language learning motivation: Pathways to the new century* (pp. 105–120). Manoa: University of Hawai'i Press.

Oller, J., Jr., Hudson, A., & Liu, R. F. (1977). Attitudes and attained proficiency in ESL: A social linguistic study of native speakers of Chinese in the United States. *Language Learning*, 27(1): 1–26.

O'Malley, J. M., & Chamot, A. U. (1990). *Learning strategies in second language acquisition.* Cambridge: Cambridge University Press.

REFERENCES

Oxford, R. L. (1990). *Language learning strategies: What every teacher should know.* New York: Newbury House/Harper and Row.

Oxford, R. L. (1993). Research on second language learning strategies. In W. Grabe, (Ed.), *Annual Review of Applied Linguistics* (pp. 175–187). Cambridge: Cambridge University Press.

Oxford, R. L. (1995). Gender differences in language learning styles: what do they mean? In J. M. Reid, (Ed.), *Learning styles in the ESL/EFL classroom* (pp. 34–46). Boston: Heinle and Heinle.

Oxford, R. L. (2003). Language learning styles and strategies: An overview. Retrieved from http://web.ntpu.edu.tw/~language/workshop/read2.pdf, November 25, 2014.

Oxford, R. L., & Burry-Stock, J. A. (1995). Assessing the use of language learning strategies worldwide with the ESL/EFL version of the *Strategy Inventory for Language Learning System*, 23(2): 153–175.

Oxford, R. L., & Ehrman, M. E. (1995). Adults' language learning strategies in an intensive foreign language program in the United States. *System*, 23(3): 359–386.

Oxford, R. L., & Nyikos, M. (1989). Variables affecting choice of language learning strategies by university students. *Modern Language Journal*, 73: 291–300.

Oxford, R. L., & Shearin, J. (1994). Language learning motivation: Expanding the theoretical framework. *Modern Language Journal*, 78: 12–28.

Padden, C. (1981). Some arguments for syntactic patterning in American Sign Language. *Sign Language Studies*, 32: 239–259.

Padden, C., & Humphries, T. (1988). *Deaf in America: Voices from a culture.* Cambridge, MA: Harvard University Press.

Padden, C., & Humphries, T. (2005). *Inside Deaf culture.* Cambridge, MA: Harvard University Press.

Padden, C., Humphries, T., & O'Rourke, T. J. (1994). *A Basic Course in American Sign Language*, (2nd ed.). Silver Spring, MD: Linstok Press.

Park, G. P. (1997). Language learning strategies and English proficiency in Korean University students. *Foreign Language Annals*, 30(2): 211–221.

Peacock, M., & Ho, B. (2003). Student language learning strategies across eight disciplines. *International Journal of Applied Linguistics*, 13(2): 179–200.

Perera, M. (2006). "Why not? But I can't"—Influence of a "culture of poverty" on learning—A case study. *Sabaragamuva University Journal*, 6(1): 23–34.

Peterson, R. W. (1999). The perceptions of deafness and language learning of incoming ASL students. *Dissertation Abstracts International* (UMI No. 9925067).

Peterson, R. W. (2009). *The unlearning curve: Learning to learn American Sign Language.* Burtonsville, MD: Sign Media, Inc.

Pfeffier, D. L. (2003). *The implementation and administration of American Sign Language programs for foreign language credit in public high schools.* (Doctoral dissertation). The George Washington University. (University Microfiche International No. 3083807). *Dissertation Abstracts International*

REFERENCES

Politzer, R. L., & McGroarty, M. (1985). An exploratory study of learning behaviors and their relationship to gains in linguistic and communicative competence. *TESOL Quarterly*, 19(1): 103–123.

Poulton, K. T., & Algozzine, B. (1980). Manual communication and mental retardation: A review of research and implications. *American Journal of Mental Deficiency*, 85(2): 145–152.

Rains, S. (2011). Deaf space: Deaf culture meets architecture in UD. Retrieved from http://www.rollingrains.com/2011/04/reprinted-with-permission-deaf-space.html, May 15, 2011.

Reagan, T. (2000). But does it count?: Reflections on "Signing" as a foreign language. *NECTFL Review*, 48: 16–26.

Reid, J. (1984). *Perceptual Learning Style Preference Questionnaire*. Retrieved from http://lookingahead.heinle.com/filing/l-styles.htm, September 5, 2011.

Reiff, J. C. (1992). *Learning styles*. Washington, D.C.: National Education Association.

Rosen, R. (2005). *National survey of high schools offering ASL as a foreign Language: Preliminary data*. (Unpublished manuscript, Teachers College, Columbia University, NY).

Rosen, R. (2006). An unintended consequence of IDEA: American Sign Language, the Deaf community, and Deaf culture into mainstream education. *Disability Studies Quarterly*, 26(2).

Rosen, R. (2008). American Sign Language as a foreign language in U.S. high schools: State of the art. *Modern Language Journal*, 92(1): 10–38.

Rutherford, S. A. (1988). The culture of American Deaf people. *Sign Language Studies*, 59: 129–148.

Sandler, W., & Lillo-Martin, D. (2006). *Sign language and linguistic universals*. Cambridge: Cambridge University Press.

Santiago, T. (2009). Children's perception of the learning of English as a second language and the textbooks used in the classroom in the colonial/postcolonial context of Puerto Rico. *Dissertation Abstracts International Section A: Humanities and Social Sciences*, 69(8-A): 2999.

Selover, P. (1988). American Sign Language in the high school system. *Sign Language Studies*, 59: 205–212.

Shams, L. (2002). Integration in the brain: The subconscious alteration of visual perception by cross-modal integration. *Science & Consciousness Review*, 1: 1–4.

Shedivy, S. L. (2004). Factors that lead some students to continue the study of foreign language past the usual 2 years in high school. *System*, 32(1): 103–119.

Shimojo, S., & Shams, L. (2001). Sensory modalities are not separate modalities: Plasticity and interactions. *Current Opinion In Neurobiology*, 11(114): 505–509.

Shroyer, E. H., & Holmes, D.W. (1982). Sign students in sign language classes. *The Reflector*, 3: 21–22.

Sign Enhancers, Inc. (1996). *Bravo ASL! Curriculum, Student Workbook, Videocourse*. Seattle, WA: Sign Enhancers, Inc.

REFERENCES

Sinnet, D. R. (1995). *An investigation of how foreign language departments at colleges and universities view American Sign Language.* (Doctoral dissertation). Florida International University. (University Microfiche International No. 9610898).

Smith, C., Lentz, E. M., & Mikos, K. (1988). *Vista American Sign Language Series: Signing Naturally*, Levels I, II and III. Berkeley, CA: DawnSignPress.

Soric, I., & Ancic, J. (2008). Learning strategies and causal attributions in second language learning. *Review of Psychology*, 15(1-2): 17–26.

Sparks, R. (1995). Examining the linguistic coding differences hypothesis to explain individual differences in foreign language learning. *Annals of Dyslexia*, 45: 187–214.

Sparks, R. (2006). Is there a "disability" for learning a foreign language? *Journal of Learning Disabilities*, 39: 544–557.

Sparks, R. (2009). If you don't know where you're going, you'll wind up somewhere else: The case of "Foreign Language Learning Disability." *Foreign Language Annals*, 42(1): 7–26.

Sparks, R., & Ganschow, L. (1991). Foreign language learning difficulties: Affective or native language aptitude differences? *Modern Language Journal*, 75: 3–16.

Sparks, R., & Ganschow, L. (1993a). Searching for the cognitive locus of foreign language learning problems: Linking first and second language learning. *Modern Language Journal*, 77: 289–302.

Sparks, R., & Ganschow, L. (1993b). The effects of a multisensory structured language approach on the native and foreign language aptitude skills of at-risk learners: A replication and follow-up study. *Annals of Dyslexia*, 43: 194–216.

Sparks, R., & Ganschow, L. (1995). A strong inference approach to causal factors in foreign language learning: A response to MacIntyre, *Modern Language Journal*, 79: 235–244.

Sparks, R., Ganschow, L., & Javorsky, J. (1993). Perceptions of high- and low-risk students and students with learning disabilities about high school foreign language courses. *Foreign Language Annals*, 26: 491–510.

Sparks, R., Ganschow, L., Javorsky, J., Pohlman, J., & Patton, J. (1992b). Identifying native language deficits in high- and low-risk foreign language learners in high school. *Foreign Language Annals*, 25: 403–418.

Sparks, R., Ganschow, L., Kenneweg, S., and Miller, K. (1991). Use of an Orton-Gillingham approach to teach a foreign language to dyslexic/learning disabled students: Explicit teaching of phonology in a second language. *Annals of Dyslexia*, 41: 96–118.

Sparks, R., Ganschow, L., & Patton, J. (2008). L1 and L2 literacy, L1 and L2 aptitude, and L2 affective variables as discriminators among high and low-achieving, learning disabilities, and ADHD L2 learners. In J. Kormos and E. Kontra (Eds.), *Language learners with special needs: An international perspective* (pp. 11–35). London: Multilingual Matters.

Sparks, R., Ganschow, L., & Pohlman, J. (1989). Linguistic coding deficits in foreign language learners. *Annals of Dyslexia*, 39: 179–195.

REFERENCES

Sparks, R., Ganschow, L., Pohlman, J., Artzer, M., & Skinner, S. (1992). The effects of a multisensory, structured language approach on the native and foreign language aptitude skills of high-risk, foreign language learners. *Annals of Dyslexia*, 42: 25–53.

Sparks, R., & Javorsky, J. (1999). Section 504 and the Americans with Disabilities Act: Accommodating the learning disabled student in the foreign language curriculum: An update. *Association of Departments of Foreign Language (ADFL) Bulletin*, 30: 36–44.

Sparks, R., Patton, J., Ganschow, L., Humbach, N., & Javorsky, J. (2006). Native language predictors of foreign language proficiency and foreign language aptitude. *Annals of Dyslexia*, 56: 129–160.

Sparks, R., Patton, J., Ganschow, L., Humbach, N., & Javorsky, J. (2008). Early L1 reading and spelling skills predict later L2 reading and spelling skills. *Journal of Educational Psychology*, 100: 162–174.

Stanovich, K. (1993). Dysrationalia: A new specific learning disability. *Journal of Learning Disabilities*, 26: 501–515.

Stewart-Strobelt, J., & Chen, H. (2003). Motivations and attitudes affecting high school students' choice of foreign language. *Adolescence*, 38: 161–170.

Stinson, M. S., & Kluwin, T. N. (1996). Social orientations toward deaf and hearing peers among deaf adolescents in local public schools. In J. Nash & P. C. Higgins (Eds.), *Understanding deafness socially: Continuities in research and teaching* (pp. 113–134). Springfield, Ill.: C. C. Thomas.

Stinson, M. S., & Liu, Y. (1999). Participation of deaf and hard of hearing students in classes with hearing students. *Journal of Deaf Studies and Deaf Education*, 4: 191–202.

Stokoe, W. C. (1960). *Sign language structure: An outline of the visual communication system of the American deaf*. Washington, DC: Gallaudet College Press.

Stokoe, W. C. (1995). Competencies important to teaching American Sign Language: Comparisons between groups. *Sign Language Studies*, 89: 303–330.

Stokoe, W. C., Casterline, D., & Croneberg, C. (1965). *A dictionary of American Sign Language on linguistic principles*. Washington, DC: Gallaudet College Press.

Sung, K.-Y. (2009). *Language learning strartegy use and language achievement for Americxan college learners of Chinese as a foreign language*. (Doctoral dissertation). The University of Texas at San Antonio. (ProQuest Digital Dissertations Accession Order No. AAT 3354825).

Tachibana, Y., Matsukawa, R., & Zhong, O. X. (1996). Attitudes and motivation for learning English: A cross-national comparison of Japanese and Chinese high school students. *Psychological Reports*, 79(2): 691–700.

Takeuchi, O., Griffiths, C., & Coyle, D. (2007). Applying strategies to contexts: The role of the individual, situational, and group differences. In A. D. Cohen and E. Macaro, (Eds.), *Language learner strategies* (pp. 69–92). Oxford: Oxford University Press.

REFERENCES

Teitelbaum, H., Edwards, A., & Hudson, A. (1975). Ethnic attitudes and the acquisition of Spanish as a second language. *Language Learning*, 25(2): 255–266.
Terstriep, A. L. (1993). Ethnicity, social theory, and Deaf culture. In J. Cebe (Ed.), *Deaf Studies III: Bridging cultures in the 21st century* (pp. 231–244). Washington, DC: Gallaudet University College for Continuing Education.
Teder-Sälejärvi, W.A., McDonald, J. J., DiRusso, F., & Hillyard, S.A. (2002). An analysis of audio-visual crossmodal integration by means of event-related potential (ERP) recordings. *Cognitive Brain Research*, 14(1): 106–114.
Teder-Sälejärvi, W. A., Munte, T. F., Sperlich, F., & Hillyard, S. A. (1999). Intramodal and cross-modal spatial attention to auditory and visual stimuli. An event-related brain potential study. *Cognitive Brain Research*, 8(3): 327–343.
U. S. Department of Education. (1992). *Policy Guidance on Deaf Students Education Services*, 57 Federal Register 49274.
U. S. Department of Education. (1999). *Analysis of Final Regulations for Part B of the Individuals with Disabilities Education Act*, 64 Federal Register 12527–12656.
U. S. Department of Education. (2006). *Educational Longitudinal Study 2002/2004* (ELS 2002/2004). Washington, DC: U.S. Department of Education, National Center for Education Statistics.
Ushioda, E. (2001). Language learning at university: Exploring the role of motivational thinking. In Z. Dörnyei, & R. Schmidt, (Eds.), *Motivation and second language acquisition*. Tech. Rep. No. 23 (pp. 93–126). Honolulu, HI: University of Hawai'i at Manoa, Second Language Teaching and Curriculum Center.
Ushioda, E. (2003). Motivation as a socially mediated process. In D. Little, J. Ridley, & E. Ushioda, (Eds.), *Learner autonomy in the foreign language classroom: Teacher, learner curriculum, and assessment* (pp. 90–102). Dublin: Authentik.
Ushioda, E. (2004). The role of students' attitudes and motivation in second language learning in online language courses. *Dissertation Abstracts International Section A: Humanities and Social Sciences*, 64(7-A): 2471.
Ushioda, E. (2007). Motivation and language. In J. O. Ostman, & J. Verschueren, (Eds.), *Handbook of pragmatics online*. Amsterdam: John Benjamins.
Valli, C., & Lucas, C. (1992). *Linguistics of American Sign Language*. (1st ed.) Washington, DC: Gallaudet University Press.
Valli, C., Lucas, C., & Mulrooney, K. J. (2005). *Linguistics of American Sign Language: An introduction*. (4th ed.). Washington, DC: Gallaudet University Press.
Van Cleve, J. V., & Crouch, B. (1989). *A Place of Their Own: Creating the Deaf Community in America*. Washington, DC: Gallaudet University Press.
Van Gurp, S. (2001). Self-concept of deaf high school students in different educational settings. *Journal of Deaf Studies and Deaf Education*, 6: 54–69.
Vandergrift, L. (2005). Relationships among motivation orientations, metacognitive awareness and proficiency in L2 Listening. *Applied Linguistics*, 26(1): 70–89.
Vellutino, F., & Scanlon, D. (1986). Linguistic coding and metalinguistic awareness: Their relationship to verbal and code acquisition in poor and normal

REFERENCES

readers. In D. Yaden & S. Templeton (Eds.), *Metalinguistic awareness and beginning literacy* (pp. 115–141). Portsmouth, NH: Heinemann.

Vernon, M., Coley, J. D., & DuBois, J. H. (1980). Using sign language to remediate severe reading problems. *Journal of Learning Disabilities*, 13(4): 215–218.

Wallinger, L. (2000). American Sign Language instruction: Moving from protest to practice. *NECTFL Review*, 48: 27–36.

Watzke, J. (1994). Why don't students study Russian? Paper presented at the annual meeting of the American Council on the Teaching of Foreign Languages, Atlanta, GA. ERIC Document Reproduction Service, No. ED378812.

Welles, E. B. (2002). Foreign language enrollments in U.S. institutions of higher education, Fall 2002. *ADFL Bulletin*, 35(2–3): 7–26.

Wen, X. (1997). Motivation and language learning with students of Chinese. *Foreign Language Annals*, 30: 235–251.

Wharton, G. (2000). Language learning strategy use of bilingual foreign language learners in Singapore. *Language Learning*, 50(2): 203–243.

Wilbers, S. (1987). The case for recognizing American Sign Language. *College Board Review*, 145: 4–9, 30.

Wilbers, S. (1988). Why America needs Deaf culture: Cultural pluralism and the liberal arts tradition. *Sign Language Studies*, 59: 195–204.

Wilbur, R. (1979). *American Sign Language and sign systems*. Baltimore, MD: University Park Press.

Wilcox, S. (1992). *Academic acceptance of American Sign Language*. Burtonsville, MD: Linstok Press.

Wilcox, S. (2014). *Universities that accept ASL in fulfillment of foreign language requirements*. Retrieved from www.unm.edu/~wilcox/UNM/univlist.html, November, 15, 2014.

Wilcox, S., & Wilbers, S. (1987). The case for academic acceptance of American Sign Language. *The Chronicle of Higher Education*, July 1, 1987: 30.

Wilcox, S., & Wilcox, P. (1991). *Learning to see: Teaching American Sign Language as a second language* (1st ed.). Washington, DC: Gallaudet University Press.

Wilcox, S., & Wilcox, P. (1997). *Learning to see: Teaching American Sign Language as a second language* (2nd ed.). Washington, DC: Gallaudet University Press.

Williams, M., Burden, R. L., & Lanvers, U. (2002). "French is the language of love and stuff": Student perceptions of issues related to motivation in learning a foreign language. *British Educational Research Journal*, 28: 503–528.

Wong-Fillmore, L. (1979). Individual differences in second language acquisition. In C. J. Fillmore, W. S. Y. Wang, & D. Kempler, (Eds.), *Individual differences in language ability and behavior* (pp. 203–228). New York: Academic Press.

Appendix A

Trends in Student Enrollment and Number of Teachers and Classes: American Sign Language as a Foreign Language

QUESTIONNAIRE

NAME OF SCHOOL: _____

RESPONDENT: _____

POSITION OF RESPONDENT: _____

I. HISTORY

1. When was the first year that classes in ASL as a foreign language were established at your school? _____

2. Please number below the order of events leading to the establishment of ASL as a foreign language classes at the school (which happened first, second, etc.). If the event did not apply or occur, please leave blank.

    _____ Teachers from other fields who know ASL and want to teach ASL as a foreign language at the school.

    _____ Students, either individually or collectively such as ASL Club, request courses in ASL as a foreign language.

    _____ Principal took the lead in creating courses in ASL as foreign language at the school.

    _____ School district requested the school to offer courses in ASL as a foreign language.

    _____ Parents requested the school to offer courses in ASL as a foreign language.

    _____ Community members requested the school to offer courses in ASL as a foreign language.

3. Please provide information below on number of teachers, classes and students, and whether students can take ASL for foreign language credit and indicate it in their transcripts for the past three years, current

Appendix A

year, and projections for next year at your school. Leave blank in certain cells if you could not answer or do not have sufficient information.

YEAR	Number of ASL Teachers, in FTE	Number of ASL Classes	Number of Students in ASL Classes	How many levels of ASL classes offered?	Is ASL given foreign language credit?
2002–2003					
2003–2004					
2004–2005 (current)					

II. STAFFING

1. Please list below the names of teachers currently teaching ASL and their highest degrees, fields, certifications (such as state teacher certification, ASLTA, etc.), and prior coursework and workshops taken.

NAMES OF CURRENT TEACHERS OF ASL	DEGREES, CERTIFICATIONS, AND EXPERIENCE	COURSEWORK AND WORKSHOPS (Please circle 'c' for coursework and 'w' for workshop. Leave blank if none)	
	Highest Degree: Field: Certifications: Years Teaching ASL: Years Teaching Other Fields:	Second Language Acquisition Linguistics of ASL Deaf Community and Culture Deaf/ASL Literature Methods and Materials in ASL Teaching Assessment in ASL	c w c w c w c w c w c w
	Highest Degree: Field: Certifications: Years Teaching ASL: Years Teaching Other Fields:	Second Language Acquisition Linguistics of ASL Deaf Community and Culture Deaf/ASL Literature Methods and Materials in ASL Teaching Assessment in ASL	c w c w c w c w c w c w
	Highest Degree: Field: Certifications: Years Teaching ASL: Years Teaching Other Fields:	Second Language Acquisition Linguistics of ASL Deaf Community and Culture Deaf/ASL Literature Methods and Materials in ASL Teaching Assessment in ASL	c w c w c w c w c w c w

APPENDIX A

Highest Degree:	Second Language Acquisition	c	w
Field:	Linguistics of ASL	c	w
Certifications:	Deaf Community and Culture	c	w
Years Teaching ASL:	Deaf/ASL Literature	c	w
Years Teaching Other Fields:	Methods and Materials in ASL Teaching	c	w
	Assessment in ASL	c	w

III. CLASSES

1. Where are the ASL classes housed in your school? Please check only one of the following.
    _____ Foreign, Modern, Second, or World Language Department
    _____ Special Education Department (such as Deaf Education)
    _____ Vocational Education Department
    _____ Extracurricular Clubs (ASL Club, etc.)
    _____ At a school for the deaf
    _____ Other: _____

2. What are the percentages of students in ASL classes in 2004–2005 who are:
    (a) Special Education students: _____
    (b) Regular Education students: _____

IV. CURRICULUM

1. Please check the following curriculum currently used by teachers in ASL-as-foreign-language courses at the school. You can check any that applies.
    _____ *Signing Naturally* ("Vista") series.
    _____ *A Basic Course in ASL* ("ABC" book) series.
    _____ *American Sign Language: A Teacher's Resource Text on Curriculum* ("Green Book")
    _____ Gallaudet University's K-12 L1 and L2 curriculum for ASL.
    _____ District-made curriculum
    _____ Teacher-made curriculum

APPENDIX A

2. What is the approach in teaching ASL used by the teachers? Please number the following in order of importance.
   _____ Sign vocabulary
   _____ Nonmanual segments and classifiers
   _____ Grammar
   _____ Conversation

V. REQUEST FOR INFORMATION

1. Is there additional information that you would like to add about the ASL program and classes at your school that is not covered in the above? We may include the additional information in this survey study.

2. Is there an ASL club at the school? If so, what are the activities?

3. Are there other secondary schools within your school district that offer ASL as a foreign language? With this information we will contact the schools(s) and send them the questionnaire.

Your kind assistance is greatly appreciated! We will send you the results of the study if requested. Please include email address since the report will be mailed via email attachment. Thank you.

Source: Rosen (2008)

Appendix B

The Study of American Sign Language as a Foreign Language

Student Demographic Information

Please put down month and day of birth:

    Month of birth: _____

    Day of birth: _____

Please circle and fill in responses:

Age: 14   15   16   17   18   19   20

Gender: M   F

Grade: 9   10   11   12

ASL Level (one level for each year):   1   2   3

ASL course: Required (Regents) _____ Elective _____

Ethnicity: White   African-American   Hispanic
            Asian   Mixed   Other

Language(s) spoken: English   Other _____

What is my first language?:   English   Other _____

Have I participated in deaf community activities?:   YES   NO

    If YES,

       How often?   0–5 times each year   more than 5 times each year

       For how many years?   0–1 year   2–4 years   5+ years

Appendix B

Reasons for Taking American Sign Language

Please check once per item.

	Very Important	Somewhat Important	Least Important	Not Important
Why do I take ASL?				
Intellectual interest in the language	___	___	___	___
Ease of learning a foreign language	___	___	___	___
Need to communicate with family and friends	___	___	___	___
Career Plans	___	___	___	___
I take ASL because:				
It is easier to learn than other foreign languages	___	___	___	___
I did not do well in other foreign languages	___	___	___	___
My guidance counselor asks me to take ASL	___	___	___	___
ASL is a unique language that I want to learn	___	___	___	___
ASL helps me learn and use English better	___	___	___	___
I want to communicate with my family	___	___	___	___
I want to communicate with my friends	___	___	___	___
I want to learn about deaf people	___	___	___	___
I want to work with deaf people in the future	___	___	___	___
I want to become a teacher of ASL in the future	___	___	___	___

APPENDIX B

I want to challenge myself in learning the language	___	___	___	___
Learning ASL helps me learn and use English better	___	___	___	___

Learning and Using ASL

Please circle one answer for each question.
  To AGREE means that you think and do that way.
  To DISAGREE means that you DO NOT think and do that way.

How does ASL (including vocabulary and sentences) appear to me?

ASL appears to consist of icons (pictures, images)	Agree	Disagree
ASL appears to consist of gestures (mimes, pantomimes)	Agree	Disagree
ASL appears to consist of English signs.	Agree	Disagree

When I learn new signs (including vocabulary and sentences), how do I think?

I think of pictures and images that describes the new signs.	Agree	Disagree
I think of actions that describes the new signs.	Agree	Disagree
I think of its English translation.	Agree	Disagree

How do I take notes of new signs to help me remember them?

I draw pictures and images that describe new signs.	Agree	Disagree
I put down actions that describes the new signs.	Agree	Disagree
I put down English words for new ASL signs.	Agree	Disagree

How much does my first language, such as English, influence my learning of ASL?

I think of English words when I learn new ASL signs.	Agree	Disagree
I think of English sentences when I learn new ASL sentences.	Agree	Disagree

During American Sign Language class, I would like:

To have a combination of ASL and English spoken.	Agree	Disagree
To have as much English as possible spoken.	Agree	Disagree
To have only ASL signed.	Agree	Disagree

APPENDIX B

I learn better when:

I give narrations	Agree	Disagree
I do dialogues with other people in class	Agree	Disagree
I follow the students' textbook	Agree	Disagree
I listen (watch) activities	Agree	Disagree
I do grammar exercises	Agree	Disagree
I play ASL games in class	Agree	Disagree
I do homework	Agree	Disagree
I do project work	Agree	Disagree
I translate from ASL to English	Agree	Disagree
I translate from English to ASL	Agree	Disagree

Whenever I don't know signs:

I ask the teacher.	Agree	Disagree
I ask other students.	Agree	Disagree
I look up in the textbook dictionary, internet, CDs, or videos.	Agree	Disagree

When I learn ASL:

I emphasize vocabulary.	Agree	Disagree
I emphasize grammar.	Agree	Disagree
I emphasize discourse.	Agree	Disagree

If I had the opportunity to use ASL outside of school, with families or friends:

I would never use ASL.	Agree	Disagree
I would use ASL.	Agree	Disagree
I would use ASL and English.	Agree	Disagree

Thank you so much for participating!!

Index

Figures and tables are indicated by *"f"* and *"t"* following page numbers.

Abo, S., 52
achievement. *See* learner achievement
ACTFL (American Council on the Teaching of Foreign Languages), 37
affective learning strategies, 50, 52, 102–3, 104, 115
age differences
    in language learner strategies, 64, 66–67*t*, 71, 73*t*, 74
    in language perceptual processing schemas, 62
    in learner achievement, 106–7, 114
    in motivation for learning ASL, 39–43, 40–42*t*, 44
Alabama, recognition of ASL as foreign language in, 8
Alexander, P. A., 93
American Council on the Teaching of Foreign Languages (ACTFL), 37
American Sign Language (ASL)
    achievement in. *See* learner achievement
    classroom language preferences for learning, 79–80, 80*t*, 88–89, 111, 123
    as foreign language, 2–4, 6–9, 8*f*
    as full-fledged language, 1–2, 3, 4
    high school programs. *See* high school ASL programs
    linguistic area of study preferences for learning, 80, 81*t*, 89–90, 112, 124
    linguistic features of, 1–2, 3, 4
    motivation for learning. *See* motivation for learning ASL
    reliance on English for learning, 78–79, 79*t*, 88, 122–23
    strategies for learning. *See* language learner strategies (LLSs)
    undergraduate programs. *See* undergraduate ASL programs
American Sign Language Teachers Association (ASLTA), 7
amplification devices, 4
AMTB. *See* Attitude Motivation Test Battery
Ancic, J., 102, 115
Anderson, J. R., 50
Arizona
    ASL course enrollment in, 12
    learning disabled students in ASL programs in, 14
ASL. *See* American Sign Language
ASLTA (American Sign Language Teachers Association), 7
assessment. *See also specific assessment measures*
    of language learner strategies, 49–50
    of learner achievement, 56, 98
    of motivation for learning ASL, 30–31, 32
Attitude Motivation Test Battery (AMTB), 30–31, 34, 35, 99, 103
auditory perceptual processing schema
    gender differences in, 53
    in general education learners, 87–88
    instructional preferences and activities, 49, 53, 54, 97, 116, 118–19
    in learning disabled students, 86, 93–94
autism, 26

INDEX

Baker, S. C., 32, 33, 44
Barbe, W. B., 49, 58–59, 92
beliefs about Language Learning Inventory (BALLI), 32, 34, 35, 49–50, 59
beliefs about Learning ASL Inventory, 32, 34, 59
Belmechri, F., 30, 34, 37
Burden, R. L., 32, 44
Burry-Stock, J. A., 50

CAL. *See* Center for Applied Linguistics
California
    ASL course enrollment in, 12
    levels of ASL classes in, 14
    recognition of ASL as foreign language in, 7
California Association of the Deaf, 7
California State University at Northridge, 7, 46
career plans, as motivation for learning ASL, 39, 43–44, 45, 46
Center for Applied Linguistics (CAL), ix, 1, 11
Chamot, A. U., 50
Chang, S. F., 52, 92
Chen, H., 43
Chen, Y.-C., 102, 115
Chen, Y.-L., 52
Chiang, H.-H., 102, 115
Chinese speakers, motivation for learning English, 100
Chou, Y.-C., 92, 103, 104, 115
Clary, W. M., Jr., 7
Clement, R., 30, 32, 33, 43, 44, 100, 115
cognitive learning strategies, 50, 52, 92–93, 102–3, 115
college ASL programs. *See* undergraduate ASL programs
communication capabilities, as motivation for learning ASL, 39, 43, 47
Connecticut
    ASL course enrollment in, 12
    learning disabled students in ASL programs in, 14
    levels of ASL classes in, 14

course level
    language learner strategies and, 69–71, 70*t*, 74, 76*t*
    language perceptual processing schemas and, 62
    learner achievement and, 106, 107, 114
    motivation for learning ASL and, 39–43, 40–42*t*, 44–45
Critz, M. A., 43
Cronbach's Alpha Test, 23, 23*n*5
Crookes, G., 31, 34, 35
Csizer, K., 33, 99, 114

Deaf, legal definition of, 4
Deaf community
    cultural traditions of, 2, 3
    integration into American society, 5
DeafSpace studies, 125
Department of Education, U.S., 5–6
differentiated instruction, 96, 118–19
Dinklage, K. T., 55
disabled students. *See* learning disabled students
discriminant analysis, 39
Donovan, L. A., 33
Dörnyei, Z., 32, 44, 53, 93, 99, 114
Dreyer, C., 101, 115
Dunn, K. J., 49, 59, 92, 93
Dunn, R. S., 49, 59, 92, 93
Dyslexia, 12

Education Department, U.S., 5–6
Education for All Handicapped Children Act (EAHCA). *See* Individuals with Disabilities Education Act of 1975 (IDEA)
Ehrman, M. E., 102, 115
Eigenvalues, 40, 40*n*6
Ely, C. M., 43
Empire State Association of the Deaf, 7
English language
    motivations for learning, 99–100
    reliance on English for learning ASL, 78–79, 79*t*, 88, 122–23
    skill improvement as motivation for learning ASL, 39, 43, 47, 125–26

INDEX

extra-linguistic features, x, 48
extrinsic motivation. *See* instrumental motivation

factor analysis, 38–39
Flemens, K., 103–4, 115
Florida
 ASL course enrollment in, 12
 learning disabled students in ASL programs in, 14
Foreign Language Learning Disability (FLLD), 56, 117
foreign languages
 ASL as, 2–4, 6–9, 8f
 characteristics of, 2, 3–4
 factors influencing learning of, x
 learning disabled students, difficulties with, 55–57
Foster, S., 31, 100, 114

Gallaudet University, 46
Ganschow, L., 56–57, 116
Gardner, R. C., 30–31, 33, 34–35, 99, 100, 101, 114
Garner, R., 93
gender differences
 in language learner strategies, 64, 68t, 69, 74, 75t
 in language perceptual processing schemas, 53–54, 63
 in learner achievement, 106, 107, 114
 in motivation for learning ASL, 32–33, 39–43, 40–42t, 44
general education learners
 achievement in ASL by, 105–12, 106t, 108–9t, 114–15, 117
 classroom language preferences for learning ASL, 79–80, 80t, 88–89, 111, 123
 language learner strategies of, 64–71, 65–68t, 70t, 74, 77–85, 79–85t, 87–91, 95–96
 language perceptual processing schemas of, 61–62, 61t, 63, 87–91, 122
 learning activity preferences of, 82–84, 83–84t, 90–91, 111

linguistic area of study preferences for learning ASL, 80, 81t, 89–90, 112, 124
 note-taking strategies of, 81, 82t, 87, 90, 111, 123
 questioning source preferences of, 84–85, 85t, 91, 111–12
 reliance on English for learning ASL, 78–79, 79t, 88, 122–23
Ghenghesh, P., 33, 44
Gobel, P., 32, 44
Grosse, C. U., 43
group centroids, 42, 42n8, 42t
Gustina, D., 31, 100, 114

Hansis, R., 93
hard of hearing, legal definition of, 4
high school ASL programs
 achievement in. *See* learner achievement
 benefits of, 45, 125
 data and statistical analysis of, 10–12, 28–29
 demographics of learners in, 19–22, 24–28, 25–26t, 27f, 28t, 149
 factors impacting achievement in, 16–17
 future research directions, 128
 general education learners in. *See* general education learners
 growth of, ix, 1
 history of inclusion in curriculum, 4–9, 8f
 language learner strategies in, 64–71, 65–68t, 70t
 language perceptual processing schemas of learners in, 61–63, 61t
 learning and using ASL, student questionnaire, 151–52
 learning disabled students in. *See* Learning disabled students
 methodology for study of, ix–x, 9–10, 17–18, 21–24
 motivation of learners in, 33, 37–45, 38t, 40–42t
 reasons for taking ASL, student questionnaire, 150–51
 recruitment of learners for, 46–47
 schools participating in study of, 18–20

INDEX

high school ASL programs (*continued*)
   teacher and school questionnaire used in study, 145–48
   teachers of. *See* teachers
Holmes, D. W., 4
Horwitz, E. K., 32, 34, 35, 49–50, 53, 59, 92
Hou, Y-A., 101, 115
Huang, S. C., 52, 92
Hudson, A., 99, 114
Hummel, K., 30, 34, 37

Illinois, ASL course enrollment in, 12
Indiana, levels of ASL classes in, 14
Individuals with Disabilities Education Act of 1975 (IDEA), 4–5, 6, 13
instrumental (extrinsic) motivation, 30–31, 52, 99–100
integrative (intrinsic) motivation, 30–33, 52, 92–93, 99, 100, 114–15
intellectual interest, as motivation for learning ASL, 39, 43, 46
internal reliability, 23, 37
interpreters, in mainstreamed settings, 6
intrinsic motivation. *See* integrative motivation
Iowa, recognition of ASL as foreign language in, 8

Japanese speakers, motivation for learning English, 100

Kang, S., 102, 115
Kemp, M., 4, 51
kinesthetic perceptual processing schema. *See* tactile/kinesthetic perceptual processing schema
Kissau, S., 32, 44
Kormos, J., 33
Kreeft-Peyton, J., 7
Kruidenier, C. B., 100, 115

Lalonde, R. N., 99, 114
Lambert, W. E., 30, 31, 34, 35
Lang, H. G., 31–32, 34, 35, 43, 44, 100, 114

language learner strategies (LLSs), 48–97
   affective, 50, 52, 102–3, 104, 115
   age differences in, 64, 66–67t, 71, 73t, 74
   assessment of, 49–50
   cognitive, 50, 52, 92–93, 102–3, 115
   course level, impact on, 69–71, 70t, 74, 76t
   defined, 48, 49
   gender differences in, 64, 68t, 69, 74, 75t
   of general education learners, 64–71, 65–68t, 70t, 74, 77–85, 79–85t, 87–91, 95–96
   learner achievement and, x, 101–4, 110–12, 115–17
   of learning disabled students, 54–58, 71–77, 72–73t, 75–76t, 85–88, 95–96
   literature review, 50–51, 52
   memory-based, 50, 52
   metacognitive, 50, 52, 92–93, 102–3, 104, 115
   methodology for ascertaining learner preferences, 58–61, 60t
   motivation and language processing predictors of, 52–54, 77–86, 79–85t, 91–93
   pedagogical implications of, 96–97
   relationship with motivation and language processing schemas, 52–54
   social, 50, 52, 103, 115
language perceptual processing schemas
   age differences in, 62
   auditory. *See* Auditory perceptual processing schema
   course level, impact on, 62
   gender differences in, 53–54, 63
   of general education learners, 61–62, 61t, 63, 87–91, 122
   learner achievement and, x, 101, 103–4, 110, 115–17
   of learning disabled students, 54–58, 62–63, 85–88, 93–94, 122
   methodology for ascertaining learner preferences, 58–61, 60t
   pedagogical implications of, 96–97
   perceptual schemas of, 48–49, 53–54

INDEX

as predictor of language learning
strategies, 52–54, 77–86, 79–85*t*, 91–93
tactile/kinesthetic, 49, 53–54, 86, 87, 93, 116
visual. *See* Visual perceptual processing schema
language processing, defined, 48
Languages Other Than English (LOTE) designation, 21–22
Lanvers, U., 32, 44
LCDH (Linguistic Coding Deficient Hypothesis), 55–56, 116
learner achievement, 98–121
   age differences in, 106–7, 114
   assessment of, 56, 98
   course level and, 106, 107, 114
   discussion of study results, 114–17
   gender differences in, 106, 107, 114
   of general education learners, 105–12, 106*t*, 108–9*t*, 114–15, 117
   language learner strategies and, x, 101–4, 110–12, 115–17
   language perceptual processing schemas and, x, 101, 103–4, 110, 115–17
   of learning disabled students, 104–5, 112, 113*t*, 116–17
   literature review, 99–104
   methodology for study of, 105
   motivation and, 30, 37, 99–101, 103–4, 109–10, 114–15
   pedagogical implications of, 118–21
Learning about American Sign Language Inventory, 50
learning disabled students
   achievement in ASL by, 104–5, 112, 113*t*, 117
   demographics of, 20–21, 25–28, 26*t*, 27*f*, 28*t*
   enrollment in ASL classes, 12–14, 13*t*
   foreign language difficulties of, 55–57
   language learner strategies of, 54–58, 71–77, 72–73*t*, 75–76*t*, 85–88, 95–96
   language perceptual processing schemas of, 54–58, 62–63, 85–88, 93–94, 122
   schools participating in study of, 19–20

learning strategies. *See* language learner strategies
linear regression analysis, 77
linguistic coding, 55–56, 116
Linguistic Coding Deficient Hypothesis (LCDH), 55–56, 116
linguistic learning strategies, 50
Liu, R. F., 99, 114
LLSs. *See* language learner strategies
LOTE (Languages Other Than English) designation, 21–22
Loux, D., 7
L2 research. *See* second language research
Lui, Y., 31, 100, 114
Lukmani, Y. M., 99–100, 114

Mabbott, A., 55
Macaro, E., 103, 104, 115
MacIntyre, P. D., 32, 33, 44
Maine
   ASL course enrollment in, 12
   levels of ASL classes in, 14
mainstreamed settings, 4–6, 5*n*2
Manually Coded English, 5
Marathi speakers, motivation for learning English, 99–100
Maryland
   learning disabled students in ASL programs in, 14
   levels of ASL classes in, 14
   recognition of ASL as foreign language in, 7
Masgoret, A.-M., 99, 100, 114
Massachusetts, levels of ASL classes in, 14
Matsukawa, R., 100, 114
McGroarty, M., 102, 115
McKee, D., 50–51
McKee, R. L., 50–51
memory learning strategies, 50, 52
metacognitive learning strategies, 50, 52, 92–93, 102–3, 104, 115
Mihic, L., 99, 100, 114
Miller, L., 31, 33, 43, 44
Minggui, G., 102, 115
Mochizuki, A., 92

INDEX

Modern Language Aptitude Test (MLAT), 56
Moorcoft, R., 99, 114
Mori, S., 32, 44
motivation for learning ASL, 30–47
  age differences in, 39–43, 40–42t, 44
  assessment of, 30–31, 32
  career plans as, 39, 43–44, 45, 46
  communication with family and friends as, 39, 43, 47
  course level, impact on, 39–43, 40–42t, 44–45
  data and statistical analysis of, 37–43, 38t, 40–42t
  discussion of study results, 43–45
  English skill improvement as, 39, 43, 47, 125–26
  gender differences in, 32–33, 39–43, 40–42t, 44
  grade level and, 33
  instrumental, 30–31, 52, 99–100
  integrative, 30–33, 52, 92–93, 99, 100, 114–15
  intellectual interest as, 39, 43, 46
  learner achievement and, 30, 37, 99–101, 103–4, 109–10, 114–15
  literature review, 30–34
  methodology for study of, 34–37, 36f
  as predictor of language learning strategies, 52, 77–86, 79–85t, 91–93
  recruitment of learners, implications for, 46–47
Mowl, G., 31, 100, 114
Mullins, P. Y., 102, 115

Naiman, N., 50
Nakayama, A., 52
National Association of the Deaf (NAD), 5–6, 7
National English Test in Proficiency for all on the Web (NETPAW), 101
National Technical Institute for the Deaf, 46
Nevada, recognition of ASL as foreign language in, 7
New Jersey
  ASL course enrollment in, 12
  learning disabled students in ASL programs in, 14
  levels of ASL classes in, 14
New Mexico, ASL for foreign language credit in, 7–8
New York
  learning disabled students in ASL programs in, 14
  levels of ASL classes in, 14
  recognition of ASL as foreign language in, 7
Nisbet, D. L., 102, 115
Noels, K. A., 30, 31, 43
North Dakota, ASL for foreign language credit in, 7–8
note-taking strategies, 81, 82t, 87, 90, 111, 123
Nyikos, M., 92

Ohio, ASL course enrollment in, 12
Okada, M., 52
Oller, J., Jr., 99, 114
O'Malley, J. M., 50
Oregon
  ASL course enrollment in, 12
  learning disabled students in ASL programs in, 14
  levels of ASL classes in, 14
Oxford, R. L., 31, 34–35, 49–50, 52–54, 59, 92, 101–2, 115

Park, G. P., 101, 115
PASW (Predictive Analytics SoftWare), 29
Pelletier, L. G., 30, 43
Pennsylvania, levels of ASL classes in, 14
Perceptual Learning Style Preference Questionnaire (PLSP), 101
perceptual processing disorders, 12
perceptual processing schemas. *See* language perceptual processing schemas
Peterson, R. W., 4, 31–35, 43–44, 50–51, 59, 92, 94, 96

INDEX

Pfeffier, D. L., 7
Pohlman, J., 116
Politzer, R. L., 102, 115
pragmatic learning strategies, 50
Predictive Analytics SoftWare (PASW), 29

recruitment of learners, motivation factors and, 46–47
Rehabilitation Act of 1973, 12–13
reliability, internal, 23, 37
research. *See* second language (L2) research
residential schools, 5
Rosen, Russell S.
    motivations for writing book, ix, x
    studies and surveys conducted by, 4, 7, 9–12

Santiago, T., 93
Scanlon, D., 55
Schmidt, R.W., 31, 34, 35
second language (L2) research
    on determinants of learner performance, 17
    on foreign language processing, 48
    growth of, 16, 30
    on language learner strategies, 50, 51
self-determination theory, 31
Selover, P., 7
Shearin, J., 31, 34, 35
Shedivy, S. L., 43
Shroyer, E. H., 4
SILL. *See* Strategy Inventory in Language Learning
Smythe, P. C., 33
social learning strategies, 50, 52, 103, 115
Soric, I., 102, 115
Sparks, R., 55, 56–57, 94, 95, 116, 117
Stewart-Strobelt, J., 43
Strategy Inventory in Language Learning (SILL), 49–50, 59, 101, 102, 103
Structure matrix, 41, 41*n*7
Swassing, R. H., 49, 58–59, 92

Tachibana, Y., 100, 114
tactile/kinesthetic perceptual processing schema, 49, 53–54, 86, 87, 93, 116
Takeuchi, O., 115
teachers
    differentiated instruction by, 96, 118–19
    pedagogical recommendations for, 96–97, 119–21, 126–27
    qualifications for, 15
Teitelbaum, H., 100, 114–15
Tennant, J., 99, 100, 114
Test of English as a Foreign Language (TOEFL), 101, 102
tests. *See* assessment
Texas
    ASL course enrollment in, 12
    levels of ASL classes in, 14
    recognition of ASL as foreign language in, 7
TOEFL (Test of English as a Foreign Language), 101, 102
Tourette's Syndrome, 26
Tremblay, P. E., 101
Tuman, W. V., 43

undergraduate ASL programs
    growth of, 1, 11–12
    language learner strategies in, 50–51
    motivation of learners in, 31–33, 44
U.S. Department of Education, 5–6
Ushioda, E., 30, 99, 100, 114, 115
Utah
    ASL course enrollment in, 12
    levels of ASL classes in, 14

Vallerand, R. J., 30, 43
Vandergrift, L., 100
Velluntino, F., 55
verbal learners, 53
Virginia
    ASL course enrollment in, 12
    levels of ASL classes in, 14
    recognition of ASL as foreign language in, 7

INDEX

visual perceptual processing schema
  in general education learners, 87–88
  instructional preferences and activities, 49, 53, 54, 97, 116, 118
  in learning disabled students, 86, 93–94

Washington
  ASL course enrollment in, 12
  levels of ASL classes in, 14
  recognition of ASL as foreign language in, 7
Watzke, J., 43
Welles, E. B., 1
Wen, X., 114

Wharton, G., 92
Wide Range Achievement Test-Revised (WRAT-R), 56
Wilcox, P., 1, 11
Wilcox, S., 1, 11
Wilk's Lambda, 40, 40n6
Williams, M., 32, 44
Wong-Fillmore, L., 50
Woodcock-Johnson Psychoeducational Battery (WJPEB), 56

Yu, J., 102, 115

Zhong, O. X., 100, 114